Vos Makhstu Y'all
The Bass Family Of North

Marcia Bass Brody and Ken Bass

Vos Makhstu Y'all
The Bass Family Of North

Foreword

It used to be that if you ordered breakfast at a southern restaurant, you'd automatically receive grits with your order. When I was growing up, folks said the letters in grits stood for "Girls Raised in the South." I was one of those girls raised in the South, having grown up in the town of North, located in rural South Carolina. I lived in North until graduating from college before my 21st birthday.

If someone asked where North was, we joked that "North is 90 miles southeast of Due West"—Due West being another little town in South Carolina. That joke got a big laugh from host Bill Cosby when I was on television's "You Bet Your Life" show in 1992.[1]

Some families have mazel (luck), and other families have challenges. I belong to the latter, having confronted challenges all my life. One challenge was when I graduated college and accepted a job in Charlotte, NC—a city where I had no relatives and knew no one. Another challenge was marrying a man from Philadelphia, and once moving there, not knowing anyone in a city where, again, no relatives from my side of the family lived. An even greater challenge arose when my marriage of 28 years ended by divorce and at age 55 I had to look for a full-time job outside of the home where I had been a homemaker for nearly 25 years. Twelve years later I was confronted with another major challenge when, at age 67, my job as a legal secretary was terminated along with those of nine other legal secretaries. They said it was a reduction in personnel, and I was told my age did not enter into the picture. I had to believe them because this was a prestigious law firm and lawyers, as we all know, never fib.

While working in Charlotte, a friend asked me if, like myself, my father had a southern accent. I answered by telling her that my father owned a dry goods store and whenever a Jewish traveling salesman came into the store, my father would say in his distinct Russian Yiddish

---

1 To see the video clip, go to: www.youtube.com/watch?v=nGRKTkS7pW8

accent, "Vell, vos makhstu, ya'll?" Vos makhstu loosely translated from Yiddish means, "how are you"?

I am the fifth of seven children born to Esther and Nathan Bass, the others being Bernie (officially Samuel Bernard), Herbie (Herbert), Ruth, Frances, Lucille, and Jack. Bernie, who died in 1985, became a lawyer and settled in Chicago. Herbie was killed in action in World War II at Guadalcanal. The American Legion Post in North is named in honor of Herbie and another boy, the town doctor's son, who were North's only two casualties of World War II. If you ever pass through North and go to the Nelson-Bass American Legion Post, you'll see my brother's picture on the wall with a write-up about him.

My youngest brother, Jack, is the author of many books on politics and history, including one that won the prestigious Robert F. Kennedy Book Award. For years I asked Jack to write a history of our family—a big Jewish family growing up in a small Southern town right in the middle of the cotton belt. He told me a 24-hour day was not long enough for all he already had to do, but that he had faith in my ability to write the story. I asked how do I begin, and he said, "Start at the beginning." So, I began to collect memories from my siblings, cousins, nieces and nephews, adding them to interviews Jack had conducted awhile back with relatives who are no longer living. I did research at the National Archives, the American Family Immigration History Center at Ellis Island, New York, and Gratz College in Pennsylvania, which has a Jewish History program.

I put everything together and then my nephew, Ken—Jack's son, who had retired young from his law practice to do some writing—volunteered to expand and edit what I'd done. The result is this book: "Vos Makhstu Ya'll: The Bass Family of North."

With our children, grandchildren, great-grandchildren, and great, great grandchildren we—the offspring of Nathan and Esther Bass—are now scattered throughout our United States. So far, there are 96 living direct descendants, with more on the way, although my generation's years are numbered. Even though we may not be close in miles, we all remain close to each other because we are and always will be family.

Marcia Bass Brody

My middle name, Nathan, is in honor of my grandfather, Nathan Bass, whom I never met. Grandpa Bass died on January 2, 1958, about ten months before I was born. We have pictures of me as an infant in the arms of Nathan's widow, my grandmother Esther Bass.

I don't remember a whole lot about Grandma either. She was very short, and pudgy, all the better to hug. One of my fondest memories is of Grandma letting me drink coffee—mostly milk and sugar, really—with my younger brother while she took care of us one weekend. I hope that's not when I started my longtime addiction to caffeine. We were staying in Grandma's home in the tiny town of North, South Carolina, while our parents were off doing something, a precious weekend for them without the kids. I felt so grown up drinking coffee—just like Mom and Dad.

For us "big city" kids from Columbia, South Carolina—the state capital, mind you—North was quite an adventure. Four blocks in one direction from Grandma's house and we'd be in "downtown" North, with its row of stores and train tracks. A block in the other direction and we'd be out in the country standing in a cotton field. In the backyard, overhung with pecan trees, we could squeeze two nuts together in one hand to crack open a tasty treat.

For us, as young kids, North was a family gathering spot, with lots of aunts and uncles and cousins. I remember once, when I was bit older, celebrating Passover at Grandma's house. There was a big crowd—for sure; my dad's three sisters from other parts of South Carolina were there, along with at least a dozen of my first cousins. While the adults were distracted with cleaning up after the Seder, I snuck a few sips of real Passover wine (the sweet Manischewitz kind) and experienced the pleasure of mild inebriation.

Unfortunately, my more lasting memories of Grandma are those of her long decline into dementia. Many times we made the trip to pay poor Grandma a visit at her tiny apartment—Grandma's condition making it impossible to stay in her home in North—a couple blocks from my Aunt Frances Ginsburg's house in Bishopville, South Carolina (about 80 miles from North and 50 miles from our home in Columbia). There was usually a large, friendly black nurse in attendance as we sat around awkwardly, smiling at Grandma while she rambled incoherently. The apartment smelled like "old people" and I was never sad to leave.

When you're a child, you accept things the way they are. So it never dawned on me back then to ask anyone how a Jewish couple from Eastern Europe ended up living in isolated North, South Carolina. Later in life, however, I did wonder. I wish my grandfather Nathan had been around to answer that and many other questions—answers to which he could've given in English, Yiddish or German. From what I've learned of him—the different languages he spoke; the egalitarian way he treated people, whether rich or poor, black or white; the successful mercantile store he ran; his habit of translating the teachings of the Torah into real life in the hardscrabble Depression-era South—I feel confident his answers would have been enlightening.

So now I'm finding out more about my grandparents' life by helping my Aunt Marcia edit and expand her book on the history of our family. As I do so, I realize how fortunate my kids are: due to divorces and remarriages (all on my side of the family), my children have six grandparents, only one of whom is deceased. Like I said, kids accept things the way they are, so my boys don't really think twice about having the extra grandparents. Both their biological grandfathers are still mentally and physically robust, with interesting and varied backgrounds.

Out of eight biological great-grandparents, they have heritages of Eastern European Jewish, Scots-Irish, Chinese, Irish, English, Scots, and Bavarian. Sadly, my wife's mother, Jodine, passed away in September, 1996, when my oldest son was only one and a half years old, and before my youngest son was born. Jodine was quite a force and they would've loved her, and she them.

But I digress—this story begins with my grandparents. It starts on the featureless plains of Eastern Europe in a time of despair and oppression for Jews.

Kenneth Nathan Bass

I. Nathan Bass In The Jewish Pale

A cruel tsar named Nicholas I ruled Russia from 1825 to 1855. He was an anti-Semite. Nicholas I introduced compulsory military service for Jews in 1827, which was enforced by seizing Jewish children as conscripts, known as cantonists. The youngest were sometimes snatched off the streets of Jewish communities by those held responsible for meeting quotas established by the Tsar. The minimum age was 12, but younger children were taken and their ages falsified. They were force-marched to the interior of Russia, where Nicholas I had preparatory camps. They were placed in barracks (cantonments) and forced by whatever means necessary to convert to Christianity. At the age of 18 they were taken into the Army for 25 years. For his virulent anti-Semitism, Russian Jews referred to Tsar Nicholas as Haman the Second--after the reviled evil Persian King in the story that animates the Jewish holiday of Purim.

Bass family oral history has it that one of the young Jewish boys taken during Tsar Nicholas's reign was Schmuel (Samuel) Baer Bass. Fortunately, Schmuel escaped soon after the march began, to be taken in by a family in Ostryn, also known as Ostryna, a village surrounded by forests at a cross-roads between the cities of Grodno and Vilna in what is now the border region of Lithuania, Belarus and Poland. The village was three miles down a narrow dirt road through the forest to Schmuel's home town of Vasiloshok.

Spared the fate of serving as a cantonist, Schmuel as an adult settled down and became a farmer. Jews were prohibited from owning land and the government barred landowners from renting land to Jews as well. Some Jews would lease individual cows from the local noblemen, who would record each day the amount of milk obtained from the cows. Other Jews, however, using false names, were able to rent entire parcels of land for farming.[2] While we don't know how he did it,

---

2 See Vasilishki portion of Shchuchin Yizkor Book (http://www.jewishgen.org/Yizkor/szczuczyn-belarus/szc177.html). The author discusses Jewish farming in the village of Ostrova, near Vasilishok.

Schmuel apparently made a successful living as a farmer on a rented parcel for some time.

While life as a Jew in nineteenth century Russia was difficult, it certainly didn't mean isolation from other Jews. Under Russian law, dating back to 1791 and the reign of Tsar Catherine II ("Catherine the Great"), Jews were allowed to settle only in what was known as the Pale of Settlement, a large geographic area of European Russia that encompassed modern day Latvia, Lithuania, Estonia, Ukraine, Belarus and part of Poland. Despite discriminatory laws and periodic violent pogroms, the number of Jews living in the Pale grew from 1.6 million in 1820 to 5.6 million in 1910. Jews were excluded, however, from some cities within the Pale, such as Kiev, unless they had special residence permits.[3] The common phrase "beyond the pale" derives from the forced Jewish settlement in the Russian Pale.

During much of the nineteenth century it was not unusual for Jews like Schmuel to live in the countryside, supporting their families with farming, despite the restrictions on owning and leasing land. In 1882, however, half a million rural Jews were forced to move into towns and townlets, known as shtetl—literally, a Jewish town. Bass family history doesn't reveal whether Schmuel Baer Bass was among those forced to move, but perhaps he was.

What we do know is that Schmuel married Laska Kasinefsky.[4] Not a lot is known of Laska's background, but she must have been a strong-willed woman. She bore six living children (another died at birth): Jacob (Yankel), Mordecai or Max (Mottel), Noah (Noach), Harry (Hetzel), Nathan (Nachum) and Ida (Haika). The last of these, Ida, came into the world in 1888, just two weeks after her father, Schmuel, died at a young age. Family history says Schmuel was 38, but he may have been a few years older.[5] In any event, when Schmuel passed on, Nathan Bass—born August 12, 1886—was only two years old.

---

3 See "The Pale of Settlement" by Alden Oreck, The Jewish Virtual Library, http://www.jewishvirtuallibrary.org/jsource/History/pale.html

4 The spelling and pronunciation of Laska's last name are a bit vague. One source has it as Kaminesky; another as Kashtinesky. On his marriage certificate, Nathan listed it as Kasinefsky.

5 If Schmuel died at age 38, then he was only five years old when the law on Jewish cantonists was repealed by Nicholas's successor, Alexander II. More likely, Schmuel was a bit older when he died. Or the story of his abduction as a child is apocryphal.

At some point—probably around 1882 when the Jews were driven out of rural areas—the Bass family settled in the shtetl of Vasilishok (Vasiliski), which was about three miles from Ostryn down a narrow dirt road through the forest. Vasilishok would have been a familiar place for the Bass family, as its thriving market is certainly where Schmuel would have gone to sell the produce from his farm labors. Traditionally, Tuesday was market day in Vasilishok. One can easily envision Schmuel getting up at the crack of dawn on a Tuesday morning, loading a cart, and heading off, perhaps with some other Jewish farmers from Ostryn, on the three mile trip into town.

Nathan Bass, however, never experienced the hardships of farm life. Instead, he was a product of the shtetl. Located southwest of Vilna (Vilnius, modern-day capital of Lithuania), Vasilishok was a mostly Jewish town of 2700 (2000 Jewish) surrounded by forests and small farming villages.[6] Accounts of late nineteenth century Vasilishok instantly evoke images of the villagers and townspeople in the great Jewish play "Tevye the Milkman" by Shalom Aleichem, later adapted for Broadway in the famous musical, "Fiddler on the Roof".

Nathan was raised by a working mother in a family with four older brothers and a younger sister. His mother, Laska, operated a bakery in Vasilishok. Whether she started the business before Schmuel died, or they operated it together after their forced relocation in 1882, we don't know. We do know that after Schmuel died in 1888, Laska managed to support her young family without ever remarrying.

A Jewish bakery would undoubtedly have been a prominent business in a shtetl such as Vasiloshok. Although there was no central marketplace in Vasilishok, as would be typical of other shtetlach in the region, the center of the shtetl—between Grodno and Vilna Streets—had two rows of wooden stores, with twenty-two stores on each row, for a total of forty-four.

> Behind the shtetl was also a horse market where horses and cattle were sold. All week, it was very quiet in the stores. Impatiently, the storekeepers waited for Tuesday, Market Day.

---

6 See Vasilishki portion of Shchuchin Yizkor Book (http://www.jewishgen.org/Yizkor/szczuczyn-belarus/szc177.html)

Every Tuesday, the peasants from the surrounding area brought their agricultural produce to sell. From their earnings, the peasants purchased all kinds of articles for their household and agricultural needs.

From the income of the Market Day, the Jews would live all week, make Shabbat, and educate and rear their children.[7]

Laska's bakery was a busy, successful business. One of Laska's grandsons, Charles Bass—born in 1900 and a son of Max Bass—recalled that the bakery "was known for miles around." According to Charles, the bakery typically had three or four employees, but none of Laska's children worked in the business as adults.

The Tuesday market days were the busiest: "All the farmers used to come from all around," Charles recounted. "I would get out of Hebrew School and for breakfast I would get an hour. I would fix myself something for breakfast and I would sit around the table with two or three women and help roll up the dough and make bobkas—twist rolls. I bet I used to twist a thousand bobkas for the time I was there. I was fast. There was nothing to it. I helped [Grandma Laska] out in those days."

---

7 See Vasilishki portion of Shchuchin Yizkor Book (http://www.jewishgen.org/Yizkor/szczuczyn-belarus/szc177.html)

Bubbe Laska Bass.

Charles's father, Max, died when Charles was only nine years old. He recalled "Bubbe Laska" as being "a little woman. She used a cane. She never walked, she always ran – fast, fast, fast. She was the nicest person." Charles grew up in a house with just three rooms. "Someone else lived in the other rooms. It had wooden floors and the kitchen didn't even have wood, it was dirt. We used to go to the end of town and get some sand in a bucket and bring the yellow sand and after we would sweep the floor we would sprinkle a little yellow sand to make it more cheerful."[8]

Like many of the shtetl in the Pale, Vasilishok was full of Jewish tradition. "On the summer days, the *mogalnik* [the Russian operated town resort in the woods] was full of Jewish vacationers. Among the beautiful pine trees, hammocks were strung. During the day, the fully packed food baskets that were brought would be emptied completely. All week long, happiness filled the *'mogilkes'* [vacationers] with laughter and good-spirited fun. Boys climbed trees, threw pinecones at one another, and rolled on the fragrant grass."[9]

Wintertime, while bitterly cold, had its diversions as well. Charles Bass recalled that "it used to get 20 below zero, and we used to go skating on the river. It was lovely!"

Laska encouraged her boys to get a good Jewish education, which appeared to be part of her family's tradition: Laska had a brother in Bialystok who was a gaon, meaning a great Torah scholar. According to Charles Bass, Laska's brother was sometimes called "the Bialystok genius." Laska kept the bakery going through many years, including the Germans' occupation during World War I. When Charles Bass left Europe for the U.S. in 1918, Laska was in her 80's and still operating the bakery. She was in her 90's when she passed away.

One of the middle children, Noah, left home at age 13 to study at the Yeshiva in Grodno. Jews had lived in Grodno, a small city about 40 miles from Vasilishok, for six centuries. Before the Holocaust, Jews comprised roughly 60 percent of the population. After Noah settled down at Yeshiva, he brought his next two youngest brothers—Harry and Nathan—there to attend cheder, the Hebrew day school. They were among the scholarship boys, who slept in a barracks type facility and ate their meals with different families who took turns feeding needy students. Nathan would, in later life, return that favor many times.

Noah became a leader in the Jewish community, making a living as a wholesale distributor of Yiddish and Hebrew newspapers for Grodno

8 The recollections of Charles Bass come from a 1976 interview conducted by Jack Bass in Kansas City, Missouri.
9 See Vasilishki portion of Shchuchin Yizkor Book (http://www.jewishgen.org/Yizkor/szczuczyn-belarus/szc177.html)

and vicinity.[10] He printed a pamphlet on the Zionist Shekel and wrote articles in the Hebrew and Yiddish language newspapers. He was a close friend of the Yiddish poet Leib Noiidus and helped him publish his works.[11] Noah also founded the Hebrew Cultural Foundation, or Tarbut, to expand educational opportunities for Jews in Grodno. He served on the City Council, annoying the non-Jewish members by insisting on speaking in Yiddish. He also was elected to the Council of the Jewish Community, a body that provided a variety of services to the local Jews.[12]

Noah also became a prominent Zionist leader. When Noah was in Yeshiva in Grodno, there was considerable division in the Jewish community between Zionists and "Bundists", the latter of whom were socialists who believed it was folly to seek the establishment of a Jewish state in Palestine.[13] Although initially attracted to the Bundist point of view, Noah was soon persuaded to join the Zionists and quickly became a leader of the movement. He was said to be honest, fair, and quick witted, disarming his opponents with humor. In one debate, when asked "what will happen if Zionism is not realized at all," Noah responded with a typical Yiddish story. When a boy in a Yeshiva came to the age where he should get married, it was suggested to him that he should meet a particular young lady. Before doing so, he was advised to get a haircut, wash up, take a bath at the bathhouse, and get a new suit. The boy asked what if after doing all that the young woman simply did not like him. The answer, as Noah told it, was "at least get a haircut anyway; get washed up anyway; brush your hair anyway; dress up like a mensch and you'll be like one of the menschen at least. If it works, it works!"[14]

---

10 See Lexicon of Yiddish Literature (New York, 1963).
11 Noah married twice, first to Pasha Kaplan, with whom he had a daughter named Dina in 1902. Dina later married Isaac Gan, settling in Palestine in 1920, where they raised a family. Noah's second marriage was to Elka Shulkies in 1912. They had two children, Martin (Motl) in 1913 and Michel in 1919.
12 See "Noach Bass," a Yiddish pamphlet published in Tel Aviv, Israel in June 1946 by friends of Noah Bass to honor him after his death in WWII. The pamphlet was translated by Rabbi David J. Radinsky of Charleston, S.C. in August 1977.
13 Ironically, Noah's second wife, Elka Shulkies, was a leader of the Bund in Grodno.
14 Noach Bass translation at p. 21.

Young Noah Bass.

As a Zionist, Noah went to Palestine in 1905, but did not stay due to health issues. He attended several international Zionist conventions, including a conference of Russian Zionists in Helsinki during October, 1906 (at the time, Helsinki was still part of Tsarist Russia). He was friends with famous Jewish Zionists David Ben Gurion (later the first Prime Minister of Israel) and Yitchak Ben Zvi (who became the second—and longest serving—President of Israel). It was a tumultuous time for Eastern

European Jews. While some, like Noah, worked to build an active Jewish intellectual and political community, and ultimately a Jewish homeland in Palestine, many others, seeking a better life, away from persistent Russian persecution, joined a massive wave of immigration to the United States. Among those who emigrated were Noah's younger brothers, Harry and Nathan, and their sister Ida.

II. The Bass Brothers Go To America

Nathan Bass came to Ellis Island December 24, 1901,[15] from Rotterdam, Holland on the vessel *NASM Steamship Amsterdam*, a year after his next older brother, Harry, had arrived.[16] They were among the two million Jews who left Eastern Europe between 1881 and 1914 to escape pogroms, restrictive decrees, and harsh government pressure that followed the assassination of Tsar Alexander II in 1881. Most came to the United States.

We don't have any record—diary entries, letters, etc.—of either Nathan or Harry's voyage to America. It was a common experience, however, from which we can imagine what it was like for a smallish, 15-year-old Jewish boy to make such a trip.

The Amsterdam was a typical steamship of its time, constructed in 1897 and plying the waters of the Atlantic between Europe and New York City. First and second class passengers on the Amsterdam would enjoy a relatively luxurious cruise across the Atlantic, taking roughly two weeks.

Nathan, however, surely would have traveled with other poor immigrants in steerage class, enduring crowded, unsanitary conditions near the bottom of the ship, where many passengers would be seasick in their bunks for two straight weeks of rough ocean passage. If he didn't already know some of the other young boys making the trip, Nathan surely met some his age, as young teens, especially those with older

---

15 He may have arrived on December 14, 1901. On his Declaration of Intention to seek naturalization, Nathan lists the date as December 24; on his Petition for Naturalization, four years later, he lists December 14, but also says he entered the U.S. on December 24.

16 The source of this information is Nathan's much later Petition for Naturalization. A review of Ellis Island passenger arrivals, however, reveals the entry of Mochem Bass, arriving from Rotterdam on August 10, 1902 aboard a vessel known as the Rijndam. Whether that was the real arrival of Nochem (Nathan) Bass, we don't know.

siblings already in the U.S., made up a significant share of the steerage class passengers on these trips.

Upon arriving in New York City, the Amsterdam would have docked at the Hudson or East River piers, where first and second class passengers would disembark and pass through Customs at the pier, after which they were free to enter the United States. Steerage and third class passengers, such as Nathan, "were transported from the pier by ferry or barge to Ellis Island where everyone would undergo a medical and legal inspection."[17]

> If the immigrant's papers were in order and they were in reasonably good health, the Ellis Island inspection process would last approximately three to five hours. The inspections took place in the Registry Room (or Great Hall), where doctors would briefly scan every immigrant for obvious physical ailments. Doctors at Ellis Island soon became very adept at conducting these "six second physicals." By 1916, it was said that a doctor could identify numerous medical conditions (ranging from anemia to goiters to varicose veins) just by glancing at an immigrant. The ship's manifest or passenger list (filled out at the port of embarkation) contained the immigrant's name and his/her answers to numerous questions. This document was used by immigration inspectors at Ellis Island to cross examine the immigrant during the legal (or primary) inspection.[18]

One of the questions Nathan would have been asked was whether he had any relatives already in the U.S., and where he would live after getting off Ellis Island. Presumably, Nathan went to live initially with his brother Harry.

Harry had arrived in New York earlier, in 1901, at the age of 19. He started working with a pushcart, then bought a horse and wagon.

---

17 See Ellis Island National Monument, "History And Culture," http://www.nps.gov/elis/historyculture/index.htm
18 Id.

Later, he purchased a sewing machine and worked in a "shop" (factory). Assiduously saving his money, Harry eventually managed to open a little candy store called "Cheap Harry's."

When Nathan arrived, he knew no English, but managed somehow to quickly learn to speak, read, and write the new language. He first worked for an Italian grocer, learning to count in Italian. He worked in a garment factory for a while. During the summers he worked for farmers in the Catskills—indeed, when he declared his intention to seek naturalization as a U.S. citizen in September, 1908, Nathan listed his residence as the Catskills town of Mountain Dale, New York. Nathan's children never witnessed it, but he later told them he knew how to milk cows, a skill he may have picked up in his shtetl days in Vasilishok, or perhaps in the mountains of New York.

Harry, Ida and Nathan Bass.

Young Nathan, however, lived mostly in Brooklyn for the next seven years. He was one of tens of thousands of Jews who poured into the borough at the turn of the century—at one point immigrants were settling in Brooklyn at the rate of a thousand per week[19]—as they fled Eastern Europe for greater economic opportunities and political and religious freedom. For most Jewish immigrants in the later waves streaming in from Eastern Europe, Brooklyn had far more appeal than the crowded tenements of Manhattan's Lower East Side. Rent was cheaper and living conditions were more amenable to a Jewish lifestyle. For Jewish immigrants, a place like the Brownsville community in Brooklyn, a popular destination for the newly arrived, had, perhaps, "the appeal of a shtetl in the countryside and offered the hope that they could once again live a traditional way of life that they longed for," including finding "a job where they would not have to work on the Sabbath and could go to shul, as was their wont."[20]

In the seven years Nathan stayed in Brooklyn—a period when he truly went from boy to man, arriving at age 15 and leaving at age 22—things would have changed dramatically as the continued surge of immigrants transformed the borough. Indeed, in time Brooklyn became home to its own crowded tenements, especially near the bridges leading into Manhattan. Meanwhile, Nathan's older brother Harry decided to leave in 1906, moving to Lowell, Massachusetts where his cousins, the Neymans, lived. He opened and closed several stores, but the one that survived—until 1968—was United Cloak – Harry Bass, Inc.

For his part, Nathan may well have preferred those summers milking cows in the Catskills, perhaps reminding him of the farming villages like Ostryn, or his growing up years in the shtetl, hanging around his mother's bakery in Vasilishok. For whatever reason, it appears Nathan yearned for the country life more than he yearned for the traditions of Jewish life, as he would soon abandon the rich Jewish culture of Brooklyn for a new beginning in a tiny town in South Carolina.

---

19 *See* Living In America: From The Lower East Side To Brownsville, Brooklyn, http://www.museumoffamilyhistory.com/lia-fles2bb.htm. Between 1899-1904, the population of Brownsville, Brooklyn, which was 95 percent Jewish, swelled from 10,000 to 60,000.
20 *Id.*

III. Go South Young Man

By 1908, Nathan Bass, like other young men of his age and station in life, was looking to get out of New York. Nathan appeared to be restless. It was September 1908 when he filed his declaration of intention to seek U.S. citizenship while working as a "merchant" in Mountain Dale. Family lore has it that soon thereafter Nathan and his first cousin, Nathan Stotsky, decided to go to Charleston, West Virginia, for the fall and winter, but ended up in Charleston, South Carolina, after buying train tickets to "Charleston" at New York's Penn Station.

Did Nathan really end up in South Carolina by accident? No one in the family seems to know what business it was that young Nathan—then age 22 or 23—and his cousin had in mind for going to Charleston, West Virginia. Indeed, Charleston, S.C. had a well-established Jewish community with a significant economic presence, whereas Charleston, West Virginia was a small town with few Jews in it. It could be that Nathan Bass simply told the story of his "accidental" arrival in South Carolina as a joke. Or, it could be that he and his cousin indeed simply walked up to a ticket window at Penn Station, asked for tickets to "Charleston," boarded their train and accidentally wound up in the historic city on South Carolina's coast.

In any event, Nathan and his cousin arrived in Charleston, S.C. in the latter part of 1908. Jews had thrived in Charleston for more than a century at that point. In 1800, Charleston had the largest Jewish population in the United States—more than 1000, at a time when New York had approximately 400. One reason for the large Jewish presence in Charleston may have been the original constitution for the South Carolina colony. Lord Anthony Ashley Cooper, leader of the eight Lords Proprietors who received the charter for the colony from King Charles II in 1663, had his secretary, a young John Locke, draft a constitution for the new territory. In one draft, Locke included language that "Jews, Heathens" and other non-believers should have a chance to acquaint themselves with "the purity of the Christian religion" and "by good usage and persuasion ... be won over to embrace ... the truth." Jews were afforded the right to vote, making Charleston the first community in the modern world to grant Jews that right.[21]

Although Charleston had a robust Jewish community, Nathan might not have been entirely comfortable there, as most of the Jews in Charleston were descended from an earlier wave of German immigration between 1815 and 1848. The German Jews, who came from smaller European farm towns, gravitated to the South, with concentrations in Charleston and Savannah. They were very different from their more newly arrived Eastern European cousins. The Germans had assimilated well into their new homeland, achieving economic success. Many of the Germans were Reform Jews who spoke English in their religious services. Indeed, the first Reform Hebrew Congregation in the United States—Kahal Kodosh Beth Elohim—was formed in Charleston in 1824.[22]

Nathan didn't stay in Charleston long. He and his cousin looked up a man they somehow knew or learned of in Sumter, South Carolina, an inland town about 80 miles from Charleston. This man, a fellow Jew who hailed from Nathan's hometown of Vasiloshok, helped them set up a store in the tiny hamlet of Pinewood, near Sumter. Nathan and his cousin operated the store during cotton season, when the local farmers would need supplies and have money. They lived in Sumter, a county seat that had a small Jewish community, although they may have stayed in Pinewood, possibly sleeping in the store, during cotton season.

While living in South Carolina, Nathan pursued his citizenship in the United States. On May 6, 1912—four years after declaring his intent—

---

21 See Eli Evans, "The Provincials, A Personal History of Jews in the South," UNC Press (2005) at 49. Evans cites Charles Reznikoff's "The Jews of Charleston" for the proposition that Charleston was the first community to give Jews the right to vote. Francis Salvador, was the first Jewish elected officeholder in America, later giving his life in the Revolutionary War. Evans at 53. (Salvador, whose Sephardic Jewish father had become an associate of the Lords Proprietors in London after moving from the Netherlands, established a 7,000-acre indigo plantation on the South Carolina frontier in what was known as "Jews land," now part of Greenwood County, S.C.) Charleston is also home to the oldest surviving Jewish cemetery in the South, the Coming Street Cemetery, with grave markers dating back to 1764. Id. at 52.
22 See Evans at 43.

the U.S. District Court in Charleston issued Nathan Bass naturalization certificate #168754, listing him as five feet two inches in height, with dark complexion, gray eyes, brown hair, a slight scar on his chin, and previously a subject of the Russian empire. His place of residence was listed as Pinewood, S.C. Nathan's Petition for Naturalization was witnessed by Alexander and Nathan Averberck, both merchants in Sumter. To prove his residence in New York during the years he lived there, Nathan submitted the names of Benjamin Edelstein, shoemaker, and Abe Brodovsky, tailor, both of New York City.[23]

Nathan's Certificate of Naturalization.

Shortly after he became a citizen, someone recommended to Nathan that the town of North would be a better place for a store. North, about 60 miles from Pinewood, was strategically located on the Seaboard Railway line in Orangeburg County and served as the commercial center for the surrounding rural countryside. Established in 1891, when three

23 See correspondence dated Feb. 10, 1912 from Bureau of Immigration and Naturalization seeking depositions to establish residency.

men—John F. North, Samson A. Livingston and George W. Pou—each donated 100 acres to form a farming village, the town was laid out around the newly built Seaboard Railroad line from Columbia to Savannah so the local farmers would have a center of commerce.[24] Because John North, a Confederate veteran, was the oldest, the town was named after him.[25]

Nathan moved to North and opened a store for the fall season. He evidently liked it because he stayed. Although Nathan Bass was in the heart of the rural South, he probably didn't feel out of place or alone. In those days, it was not at all unusual for small southern towns to have a store owned by a Jewish family. As one writer described it of a similar establishment in rural Tennessee, "[a] Jew store—and that is what people called it—was a modest establishment selling soft goods—clothing and domestics (bedding, towels, yard goods)—to the poorer people of the town—the farmers, the sharecroppers, the blacks, the factory workers."[26] In North, they didn't call it a Jew store, but Nathan's outlet was similar, catering to poorer members of the community—tenant farmers, sharecroppers and a few land-owning yeoman farmers, both black and white.

Although at the time Nathan was the only Jew living in North, there were other Jewish immigrant merchants like him in nearby small towns. For recreation, Nathan played penny poker with many of them on Sundays, a day when their stores followed the pattern of other store-owners by closing on the Christian Sabbath. A Jewish merchant could ill afford to offend his devout Protestant neighbors and customers by opening on that day; by the same token, he felt that he could never make it in business if he closed on Saturday—the Jewish Sabbath—as that was when farm families came to town to shop.

---

24 The train made a lot of noise as it passed through North at 6 a.m. every morning. The story went that it was too early to go to work, but too late to go back to sleep, which was why people in town had large families.

25 By then he was known as "Colonel North." In the Civil War, North was a lance corporal in the Confederate Army who served as a prisoner of war for ten months. No doubt, he became a "colonel" later, as a member of the Confederate Veterans Association.

26 Stella Suberman, "The Jew Store," Algonquin Books (2001) at 3. Suberman's book is the fictionalized, heartwarming story of her father's dry goods store in a small town in Tennessee.

Apart from the tradition of the small town merchants sometimes referred to as the Country Jews, which invariably were run by Eastern European Jews, descendents of some German Jews who had settled earlier owned larger, more upscale, stores in the cities. Towns like Pinewood and North may have reminded Nathan of Vasilishok. Like Vasilishok, North was in a decidedly rural area. The hamlets of Woodford and Livingston, which fed into the North school system, were located about four miles respectively north and south of the town, also in Orangeburg County. They may have reminded Nathan of Ostrova in the old country.

There's a good chance that Nathan felt at least as much at home in North as he did in Brooklyn. Like the land in the Pale, the area around North was flat and largely featureless, except for small farms and large forests. Like the peasant farmers of Russia, the black and white sharecroppers and tenant farmers who raised cotton were poor, but they came to town to shop, especially during the fall cotton harvest. Nathan's customers also consisted of a few land-owning yeoman farmers, white and black, with large families to clothe. And like the farming areas of Eastern Europe, many of the merchants in South Carolina's other small towns were also Jews.

North was also fairly isolated from any large cities. Fourteen miles from North was the town of Denmark (named for the Denmark family), which, with a population growing to several thousand, quickly became the largest town on the 150 mile stretch of highway between Columbia and Savannah. Between Denmark and North was the small town of Norway, which got its name in an effort to create a tourist attraction by its proximity to Denmark. Between Norway and the farming hamlet of Livingston was another hamlet, Neeses, reportedly named for a Mr. Neese (probably Kneece) who had a vision from God to form a town there. (In 1940, a concerned farmer came into Nathan's store, saying that he'd heard on the radio that the Germans had "done took Denmark and Norway," adding, "and I reckon they'll be in Neeses next.").

The analogy to life in Vasiloshok is far from perfect, however: for one thing, the summer climate in North would have seemed brutally hot compared to Vasilishok, while the winters would have been far milder. For another, the existence of a large population of African-Americans— then called "colored people" in polite company—and the segregated life they led in the South would also have been something new, although Nathan could very well have identified with the discriminatory treatment meted out to Negroes, similar to that accorded to Jews in the Pale. But the small town Jews in the South—the "country Jews"—were generally accepted as white and as people of the Book—the Old Testament familiar to their overwhelmingly Baptist and Methodist neighbors (no Catholics lived in North at the time, nor were there any Episcopalian, Presbyterian, or Lutheran churches there).

While North may have physically reminded Nathan of Vasilishok, culturally it was a world apart. Vasilishok was a Jewish town, so when growing up there, Nathan would have been surrounded by Jewish families and their children. Jewish learning, traditions and culture were part of everyday life in Vasilishok, whereas in North, Nathan would be largely isolated from other Jews most of the time, except for the Jewish traveling salesmen for wholesalers who supplied the merchants. Even Brooklyn, while a crowded cacophonous city, at least had afforded Nathan the comforting blanket of Jewish life, family and friends.

Whichever way it was that Nathan came to South Carolina—accidental, or with purpose—it's clear that small town life in the rural South suited him. Nathan still made annual trips to New York, to purchase merchandise and see family and old friends, so he could easily have given up on the Southern venture at any time, but he didn't.

One thing Nathan wouldn't find easily in the small towns of South Carolina, however, was a Jewish, single woman. And so it was that Nathan, on one of his periodic buying trips to New York, in 1916, followed the suggestion of one of his cousins to meet a petite young Jewish woman he might be interested in.

IV. Esther Cohen

Esther Cohen was born around Purim, 1889 in Bialystok, Poland to Moishe and Raisel Wasserman Cohen. Because their daughter was born on Purim, she was named after the heroine of the Purim story, Queen Esther. Later she chose March 15 as her English birthday.

Compared to Vasilishok, Bialystok was a big city, a center of Jewish intellectual life in the Pale, not that Esther lived there long enough to really remember it. In 1891, when Esther was two years old, she sailed to America with her parents and her five-year-old sister, Feige. When they arrived in New York, her paternal aunts, already in the country, changed the newcomers' names so they wouldn't seem like "greenhorns" in America. Moishe became Morris; Raisel became Rose; Feige to Fanny; and Esther to Emma. When Esther married, she decided to use her given Biblical name again.

Esther's mother, Rose, was an orphan who once served as governess for a wealthy Jewish family. She could read Hebrew, knew a smattering of French, and was an educated, religious Jewish woman. In America she lived her Judaism: she visited the sick; she gave and collected charity; she took food to the needy before Shabbos (Sabbath).

Esther's father, Morris, was a master carpenter. After coming to America, Morris and Rose Cohen had three more children: Sadye, Jack and David.

The Cohens initially lived on the teeming lower east side of Manhattan, in a tenement above a brothel. As Morris developed his trade on the way to becoming a small contractor, and as Rose no doubt noted the many unescorted men visiting women in the rooms below, the family soon moved.[27]

---

27 Jack Bass and Marcia Brody, interview with Fanny Cohen Slomin, 1982.

The Cohen Family (from L-R): Rose, Jack, Fanny, David, Morris, Esther. Sister Sadye is missing.

Esther received little formal education. She dropped out of school after the fourth grade because of digestive problems, likely due to an undiagnosed congenital hiatal hernia. She began work early in life, spending years as a trusted employee of jewelry wholesaler Goldsmith Stern, for whom she delivered valuable jewelry throughout Manhattan. Her work helped put her two younger brothers through high school.

The Cohens, perhaps because they were early immigrants, seemed to live a comfortable lifestyle—by the standards of the era—at least by the time Esther was grown. She had friends at work – Jewish and non-Jewish—who she would join on occasion for the theater, classical concerts, and outings at the beach.

Having come to America at age two, Esther was probably more Americanized than many of the immigrants who followed her. Despite her lack of formal education, she had steady work in New York, such that she could afford to be a single, young Jewish woman living in the city. Being single and young as a woman is one thing. But by 1916 Esther had turned 27 years old, an age when most women of the day were married. Fortunately, Esther was about to meet an earnest young Jewish man who just happened to run a mercantile store in the tiny little southern town of North, South Carolina.

V. Nathan And Esther

The year was 1916. Europe was at war—the French and English fighting the Germans and Austrians, bogged down in a horrific battle of attrition fought in muddy trenches. The United States still hadn't entered the fight, and many Americans thought they shouldn't—it was Europe's war, after all, not much different from centuries of previous warfare on the continent.

Nathan by now was settled in North, successfully running his own mercantile—or "dry goods"—store. He'd now been in South Carolina for eight years. As he did each year, Nathan made a trip to New York, mainly to purchase merchandise for his store, but also, of course, to see family and old friends. Despite the penny poker games with other Jewish immigrants to South Carolina, Nathan must have felt pretty lonely at times.

On this particular trip to New York, Nathan eagerly took up a cousin's invitation to meet Esther Cohen (who at the time still went by the name Emma). They were well-matched, not the least because Esther was a good four inches shorter than the five foot, three inch tall Nathan. Almost four years older and turning 30, Nathan apparently was ready to settle down and start a family. In any event, they hit it off well, going out several times during Nathan's week in the City. Esther's independence no doubt impressed Nathan, and she surely enjoyed the interest he'd shown in her, although we have to wonder what Esther thought about getting involved with a man who'd decided to put his stake down in a small rural town in South Carolina.

At the end of his whirlwind week in New York, Nathan told Esther he was going back to his store, but that she would hear further from him. If ever there was a sign of how much Nathan enjoyed living in small town South Carolina, this was it. He could just as easily have lingered in New York, or even decided to sell his store and move back, to be with Esther and various relatives. Instead, he returned to the hot, dusty town in the middle of the cotton fields, still alone.

True to his word, Nathan did return to New York the following year. Before he left, he told people in North he would return with a wife. No correspondence between them, if any, survives, but imagine Esther's surprise and delight when the earnest young man from South Carolina arrived again at her doorstep after nearly a year away.

It was 1917. Nathan stayed in New York eight days that year. He took Esther to Coney Island and promenaded her on the beach, along a path on which he had cousins—Edelsteins and Brodofskys, the family names of men married to Nathan's paternal aunts—staked out under beach umbrellas to look her over.[28] They must have approved, for he asked Esther to marry him, while telling her it would have to be soon.

Esther's sister, Fanny, also approved. She and other family members viewed Nathan as a "man of the world" because "he traveled." Nathan told Esther's mother, Rose Cohen, that the wedding should be simple, that he would not have many guests. He invited his "mishpocha"—his extended family and friends from Vasilishok—and his close business acquaintances. They married in Esther's family home on August 12, 1917, with guests overflowing into the street. Nathan, at age 31, was prematurely gray, which may have made him look more mature despite his small size, while Esther was a youthful looking 27-year-old.

Happy as she was for her daughter, Rose Cohen cried, because her daughter was leaving for "the wilderness," and Rose wondered what would become of her future grandchildren. Indeed, we can only imagine what Esther, and especially her family, thought about the prospect of her moving from New York to North, South Carolina. After all, unlike Nathan, Esther had never lived in a small town, or in a community where she would not have been surrounded by Jews and their traditions. Love conquered all, however, as Esther gathered up her meager belongings, joining Nathan on a trip that would surely change her life. They honeymooned on a cruise ship to Savannah (no steerage class this time!), then took the 100-mile train ride up to North. One can only imagine Esther's

---

28 According to one recollection, they both had cousins out looking them over that day, on opposite sides of the path.

thoughts as the train crossed through the flat cotton fields with their ramshackle farm houses, rumbled through the small towns in the dead heat of late summer, and pulled into the small station at North, a town unlike any she'd ever seen before, but where she was now expected to make her home.

Nathan and Esther's marriage certificate.

When they arrived in North, the new couple took up residence in the Culler boarding house, where Nathan had been staying. Mrs. Culler served meals family style, but knew not to serve the Basses "hog meat" or to fry their eggs in bacon grease. They later moved to an upstairs apartment in the Reeds' home, and after that to a small house next door to the Methodist parsonage, where Esther became a confidant of the minister's wife, Mrs. Grier.

Nathan and Esther.

Esther soon, however, was not the only young Jewish woman in North. Shortly after Nathan returned to North with Esther, his younger sister, Ida, moved in with them. It would be interesting to learn more about the relationship between Esther and Ida, who were just about the same age. On the one hand, Ida's presence, at least early on, may well have been a comfort to Esther, who would have found it difficult to find much in common with the other women living in and around North. On the other hand, there was the usual tension of having two women sharing one kitchen in those days. Ida was a fastidious housekeeper, a good cook, but a bit imperious, whereas Esther, the longtime single city girl with a regular job in New York, had not learned to cook or keep house before she married. One suspects the relationship was complex—and strained. Not only for them, but Nathan, too, in his competing roles as husband and devoted older brother.

In the larger world, the United States had finally entered the "Great War" in Europe against the German Kaiser and his allies, formally declaring war in April, 1917. Of perhaps greater interest to Nathan, Esther, and Ida, revolution had broken out in Russia, where they still had many relatives. Many Jewish intellectuals were active in the Bolshevik movement, such that when the revolution succeeded Jews played an active role in the new government. A great flu pandemic—estimated to have killed between 50 million and 100 million around the world—was also stirring. Life in North, however, centered around the store and a growing family.

VI. A Family Grows In North

It didn't take Nathan and Esther long to get started on a family. On May 18, 1918—exactly 40 weeks after marrying Nathan[29]—Esther gave birth to the first of her seven children, Samuel Bernard Bass, named after his deceased paternal grandfather, Schmuel Baer. Bernie, as he was known, wasn't born in North. Rather, Esther returned to Brooklyn, at her mother's insistence, to have her first child.

When Esther's mother, Rose, made her first visit to North a few months after the marriage, she observed the presence of a large population of black descendants of African slaves. They mostly sharecropped cotton, which dominated the local economy, on marginal plots of land around North. Many were Nathan's customers.

Although Rose was religious and educated, she was nonetheless superstitious. Here her daughter lived in this alien landscape, pregnant with child. Rose said to Esther in Yiddish, "what you look at when you are pregnant affects your baby." She worried that Esther would give birth to a black child if she stayed in North, and so insisted that she return to Brooklyn for the birth.

---

29 One of the relatives gave Esther a present, and on the card counted the nine months from their marriage to Bernie's birth.

Ester's mother: Rose Wasserman Cohen.

During this period, it was not unusual for various relatives to visit North and stay with the Bass family for extended periods of time. The 1920 census lists in the Bass household Nathan, Esther and Samuel, but also Esther's brothers Jack (age 19) and David (age 20) Cohen, along with a servant named Edna McFadden.[30] David Cohen met his eventual wife, Janet Pearlstine of St. Matthews, while in South Carolina, and Jack Cohen later said that some of his happiest, most carefree years were spent in North.

---

30 See Fourteenth Census record for North Town, Orangeburg County, S.C.

Soon after Bernie came Herbert, born on December 27, 1920, also in Brooklyn. After that, Grandma Rose must have relented—or perhaps Esther, with two young boys to attend to at home and tired of trekking to Brooklyn on a train when heavy with child, finally put her foot down after no doubt noting that the other white women in North weren't having black babies. The boys soon had two sisters, Ruth, born in North on May 28, 1923, and Frances, also born in North, on April 15, 1925.

One suspects that the early 1920's were a good time to start a big family, as the U.S. economy boomed following the end of the Great War. In 1924 Nathan ran a half page ad in the North High School Annual for "N. Bass & Co., The Home of Satisfaction." The ad said "we are delighted to serve you at any time" and promoted the store's sale of "dry goods, ready-to-wear, notions, and shoes." Business was sufficiently good that the reader was invited to visit "our new quarters" in the Leysath Building next to the Bank of North.[31] Nathan must have worked hard in the store while Esther worked equally hard in the home, raising four young children, while helping out in the store, too. When Frances was born on April 15, 1925, Bernie, the oldest, would have been just shy of his seventh birthday.

Esther would never lose her Brooklyn accent. She would talk to customers in the store, and they would nod their heads politely, as one does in the South, saying "yes ma'am, yes ma'am." Then they'd turn to a friend, or another local, and ask "What did she say?" No doubt Esther had a similar reaction when she first heard the local Southern drawl.

Over time, the relationship between Esther and her sister-in-law Ida generated sufficient friction to prompt Nathan to do something about it. He arranged for a Jewish man named Victor Robin, whose background included time as a merchant seaman, to come to North, paying Victor's train fare. Tall, husky, and unshaven, Victor arrived as a potential suitor for Ida, clad in a shirt that had seen better days and trousers that ended inches above his ankles. Nathan met him at the train station, hustled him across the railroad tracks to the store, measured him, pulled a suit off a rack, marked it for alterations and then rushed it to the seamstress. Meanwhile, he sent Victor to the barber shop for a shave and a haircut.

---

31 North High School Annual, 1924, p. 49.

Retrieving the suit in less than an hour, Nathan drove the now neatly dressed and groomed visitor with an outgoing personality home to meet his sister Ida. The plan worked—they hit it off and soon were married, almost certainly by Rabbi David Karesh of the Beth Shalom (House of Peace) Orthodox synagogue in Columbia. Ida and Victor settled in St. Matthews, a larger town (and Calhoun County seat) about 20 miles from North,[32] where Ida soon gave birth to their first child, a girl they named Esther. She wasn't named for Ida's sister-in-law down the road in North—Jewish tradition prohibits naming a child after someone still living.

Initially, Nathan helped set Victor up with a store in St. Matthews, also called N. Bass & Co. Victor was making steady progress until the High Holy Days—Rosh Hashonah and Yom Kippur—came up. Unlike the several other Jewish merchants in town, Victor kept his store open. The Christian community viewed this as a failure by Victor to respect his own religion. Business dropped off and the new store eventually failed. Little Esther might have spent many an hour with her cousins in North, but Victor moved the family to South River, New Jersey, where he started a new store. There, the Robins had a second child, Miriam.[33]

While much of the U.S. saw good economic times until the end of the 1920's, the force of events beyond anyone's control brought about startling change in the South much sooner. By the mid-1920's, the boll weevil—a tiny beetle that feasts on cotton bolls, the green pods that develop from flowers and open into white fluffs of cotton in late summer—had moved into South Carolina after already devastating cotton crops in states to the south and west. The weevil, entering the cotton boll weeks before maturation, ingests all the nutrients and leaves a shriveled worthless interior in a dead boll.

The boll weevil's arrival brought economic devastation to cotton communities throughout the South, several years ahead of the

---

32 St. Matthews also supplied a bride to Esther's brother, David Cohen (who later changed his name to David E. Cohn, making a middle initial with the dropped letter "E"), when he married Janet Pearlstine.

33 Esther married Al Kaminsky and had two children, Ellen and David, who both live in Maryland. David is an attorney. Ellen, a teacher, and husband Les Cohen have two children, Jonathan, an attorney, and Amanda. Miriam married Jonah Greyson and they had two sons, Sam and Joshua. Sam, an attorney, lives in California with his wife Laurie and their son Marco.

Great Depression. North was not spared. Nathan, who was well-read, might have seen it coming, as the boll weevil marched across the South at the rate of about 140 miles per year, leaving devastation in its path.

There was no stopping the menace, however. The boll weevil's advance soon ended a period of economic success for Nathan, who, with his cousin Nathan Stotsky owned stores in the small towns of Johnston, Wagner and Salley, as well as the somewhat larger county seat town of Saluda, where Nathan and Gussie Stotsky lived. With a large family to support and the local cotton economy in ruins, Nathan was also forced to abandon his store in North.

By 1927 the Bass family was living in Morristown, New Jersey, where a fifth child was born on August 22, 1927. The name on her birth certificate was Mildred Bass; however, at the age of four or five she decided she did not like the name because of teasing from her sisters. She insisted that she wanted it changed to Marcia, the Jewish name her mother had given her after her recently deceased grandfather Morris. After much crying and persistence, Marcia won out. She was henceforth called Marcia even though her birth certificate still says only Mildred Bass.

Things weren't much better in Morristown. Soon Nathan moved the family again, this time to Lowell, Massachusetts, where his brother Harry had his own store and family by that time.[34] As of the 1930 census, the Bass family was living in a rented dwelling on School Street in Lowell.[35] Nathan's young family continued to grow with the birth of a sixth child, Lucille, on June 1, 1930. Lucille's Hebrew name was Laski, after Nathan's mother. The fourth daughter in a row, Lucille was born prematurely, while Esther was taking a bath, weighing in at just three pounds.

By now the Great Depression was taking hold and times were tough everywhere. Nathan must have still had fond memories of his times in North, because when a friend wrote to him, shortly after Lucille's birth, to say that he believed North could now support another store, Nathan

---

34 Harry had married Freda Rosengard, with whom he had two children, David and Lilly. Tragically, Freda died in childbirth, a not uncommon occurrence in those days. Harry later remarried, to Annie (Kaplan) Cohen, a widow herself, who already had two children, Harold and Ruth. Harry and Annie had two more children, Saul and Bette.
35 See Fifteenth Census, Lowell City, Middlesex County, Massachusetts.

returned. On Independence Day—July 4, 1930—Nathan completed a drive back to North with the older children, Bernie, Herbie and Ruth. Ruth, the youngest of those three, at age seven, later recalled being surprised that there was no Fourth of July parade in town that day. A couple weeks later Esther followed by train, bringing Marcia and Lucille, who were able to travel for free because the railroads did not charge a fare to passengers under six years old. Frances, however, at age five, had pleurisy, and was still in the hospital in New York. She recalls her cousin Bette Bass (daughter of Harry Bass) bringing her a black doll "that I loved" while in the hospital. Frances joined the rest of the family later in the summer.

Nathan's friend was right—North could support another store, despite the difficult times, at least enough so that the large Bass family could live what would have been a relatively comfortable existence for that time and place. The new store was Bass Mercantile Co. The return also reunited the Bass family with the childless Stotskys, who had remained in Saluda, roughly 40 miles from North. For years there were regular visits between the families for Sunday card games and conversation.

On June 24, 1934, the final Bass child, Jack, was born. It was the same year the oldest child, Bernie, graduated from high school and enrolled at the University of South Carolina in Columbia. This time Esther made the trip to the Baptist Hospital in Columbia, the state capital approximately 30 miles from North. Ruth, who was embarrassed that her mother was having a baby at age 45, recalls waking up in the middle of the night as Esther called the local doctor, Dr. Nelson, to tell him she was ready to go to the hospital. Talk about house calls—he picked her up in his car and drove her to Columbia! Esther announced the birth to her family by inscribing on the envelope flap of letters to Brooklyn: "J.B., 6-24-34." Now complete, with seven children—three boys and four girls—the Bass family had become well established in North.

VII. At Home In North

The 1930's represented tough times in the South as the Great Depression continued to rage. Except for brief periods of good prices for cotton, South Carolina had been a poor state ever since the devastation of the Civil War, but the Great Depression caused things to go from bad to worse. Farms went under, economic activity was sluggish, unemployment high. African-Americans, whose economic opportunities always had been limited, continued an outmigration along railroad routes to northern states that had accelerated in the 1920's and 1930's.[36] Whites, many relegated to marginal share-cropping and tenant farming, migrated from the country into cities in search of better opportunities. Jews also left the state: between 1937 and 1948, the Jewish population of South Carolina declined from 5,905 to 3,780, a precipitous decline no doubt brought about by the lengthy economic hard times.[37]

During this period, many families struggled just to put food on the table. The town of North, although recovering from its ordeal with the

---

36 The life of North's most famous African-American citizen, actress/singer Eartha Kitt, is illustrative of the racial disparities of the time. Allegedly conceived of a rape of her mother by a white man, Eartha was born near North on January 27, 1927. The Kitt name came from Laurence Keitt, a former congressman who died as a Confederate army colonel, and who was the master of the plantation on which her mother's forbears likely were slaves. Eartha was raised in a tenant farmhouse between North and St. Matthews, (served by a North rural mail route), by her mother's sister, who Eartha thought was her own mother. Eartha was abused by a local family her aunt entrusted to watch over her. When she was eight years old, Eartha was sent to New York to live with the woman she came to believe was her biological mother, and there started her ultimately famous entertainment career. See "Eartha Kitt," Wikiipedia, http://en.wikipedia.org/wiki/Eartha_Kitt (accessed 11/24/08) and Jack Bass interview with Eartha Kitt's aunt. (Jack attended three live performances by Kitt in San Francisco , Boston , and Charleston.).

37 See Evans, The Provincials, at 370 (Appendix C—"Shifts in Jewish Population in Southern States, 1937-2000). Today there are nearly 14,000 Jews in South Carolina. See Jack Bass and Scott Poole, "The Palmetto State: The Making of Modern South Carolina," University of South Carolina Press (2009) at 198.

cotton boll weevil, continued to suffer from low prices for cotton. The town wasn't growing. Between 1920 and 1940, South Carolina's population grew by more than 200,000—a 13% increase—while rural Orangeburg County, where North was located, declined by 1,200 residents (a 2% decrease).[38] The Bass children remembered young blacks regularly departing on the local Saturday train stop in North to transfer in Columbia to the Seaboard New York bound Silver Meteor. Franklin Roosevelt's New Deal provided cotton stamps to farmers who reduced cotton acreage for mandated control of production to support better prices for their crops. Despite the hardships, the Bass family was relatively well-off, perhaps because Nathan sold a full range of dry goods—primarily inexpensive clothing for the entire family—all with good service.

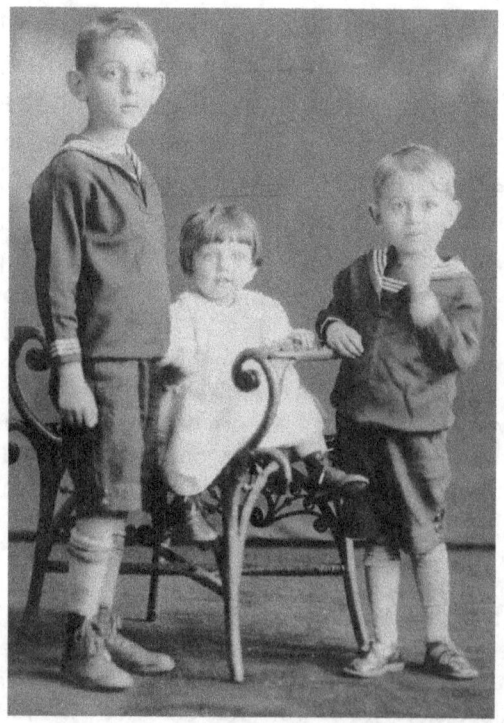

Bernie, Ruth and Herbie in 1924.

38 See "SOUTH CAROLINA, Population of Counties by Decennial Census: 1900 to 1990" (3/27/95)(http://www.census.gov/population/www/censusdata/cencounts/files/sc190090.txt (accessed 11/20/08).

After returning to North, Nathan was always able to provide his large family with a good home. The Bass family's first home was on a slight hill a block off the new highway that ran west to Augusta, Georgia. After that, the Bass family moved to a brick bungalow with a filling station on the side of the front yard and the railroad tracks across the highway. Marcia remembered that house for the chickens and ducks that roamed through the backyard. After Esther called the name of each child for dinner, a duck would also respond, quacking up to the door.

Finally, the family settled into its last home in North, a corner lot facing Bedford Avenue—the street leading to what was known as the "colored" schoolhouse, the segregated school for black children in the community. This home had a long hall going through with a bedroom in the front until Esther, who saved her money in a sugar bowl tucked away in a china cabinet, had enough money to change the layout, shortening the hall. To the right, off the shorter hall, was the dining room, and behind it, on the back of the house, the kitchen with a small back porch attached to it. To the left of the entrance hall was the front room (living room), behind which were three bedrooms. The first bedroom was Esther and Nathan's, through which one entered a full bathroom. The second was for the girls, and the last, located where the kitchen had been in the old layout, was Herbie's, and later Jack's. It opened to a half bathroom, with a larger door opening to a big screened porch with some closets.

The house was fronted by a large, inviting porch, which in later years hosted many grandchildren, who loved to climb in and out of its windows into the living room and dining room. Outside, in back, was a cellar and a long shower house, along with a "smoke house," which later got converted into a one bedroom apartment for Bernie.

The home was heated with fireplaces at first, later with space heaters. Although winters in South Carolina are mild, it could still get pretty cold, especially in January and February, when temperatures sometimes dipped below freezing at night. The girls were often chilly during these times. They would keep warm at night by snuggling with each other, two to a bed. They also took turns warming their feet with the one hot water bottle Esther had for them to share.[39] To the children's amuse-

---

39 Many years later, Ruth's husband joked that it took thirty years of marriage for her feet to get warm from the cold nights in North.

ment, one of the family's maids would sometimes lift her dress from the rear and back up to the open flame in the fireplace for warmth.

In the back yard, seven towering pecan trees provided ample shade and, in late fall, a steady supply of the delightful nuts enjoyed by generations of Basses. All the Bass children and grandchildren became adept at cracking the brown kernels and extracting the sweet nut meat inside. They were also a source of spending money for the children—Esther paid the children two cents a pound to gather the pecans, which were stored in a cellar with a dirt floor before much of the harvest was shipped off to relatives in the North, who surely saw them as an exotic treat. When he was old enough, Herbie would climb up the trees, stand on one limb at a time, and spring up and down to shake the ripe pecans loose from their casings and fall to the ground, where the younger children scooped them up by hand into a paper bag.

Jack, Lucille, Marcia, Ruth, Miriam Robin, Frances.

Across the side street lived Mr. and Mrs. Perry Adams, who owned a wind-up Victrola that played round cylindrical recordings—the Bass children's favorite was "Casey Jones." Mrs. Adams was an energetic older woman with a beautiful flower garden in which she grew brilliant orange and red poppies, while Mr. Adams was the town's lone police-man. One day, Lucille fell asleep while in the Adams home listening to records on the Victrola. When she awakened, she found out that Mr. Adams had been out with a search party combing the town for her.

Next door, on one side, were Miz Mildred and Mr. John Livingston, with their daughters Thelma and Shirley. Then there was a vacant lot used for gardening, and on the corner sat the home of the Eugene Liv-ingstons (recall that one of North's three founders was Samson Living-ston, so there were a lot of Livingstons in town)—Gene, Miz Annie and their five children, the youngest of whom was Annie Bruce, who went by Bruce and was Ruth's dearest friend growing up.

One amenity of the Bass home was indoor plumbing, which wasn't always the case in town, and a rare sidewalk in front and on the side. One of the neighbors for many years had an outhouse, and Marcia could recall watching friends bathe in a large washtub on Saturday night with water heated up by their mother on the wood stove. Likewise, the Adams family, across the street, had no running water in their home and pumped theirs from a well.[40]

The Bass home also had one of the town's few street lights in front of it, such that the children of the neighborhood would congregate there at night to play games. In a generation before television that couldn't even conceive of a computer game, the Bass children played cards, hop scotch, red rover, hide and seek, and tag. "We were able to run around town freely—never worrying about safety," Frances recalled.

The Bass family was among the early ones in North to have a tel-ephone. Most people probably didn't see much use for what, at the time, was considered an extravagant communications tool, but with a house full of kids at one end of town and a store six blocks away, having a telephone was quite a convenience for Nathan and Esther. The phone number for the store was 5-2, and for home it was 7-3. If Esther wanted to reach Nathan, however, she'd more likely simply pick up the phone

---

40 Mr. Adams was the town's lone police officer.

and give it one crank, or ring—and someone answered at the store. Two rings and someone answered at the house. Three rings and the operator answered—rather than just listening in.

The telephone operator was a ubiquitous presence in those days. Once, during World War II, Ruth called the store from Columbia, where she was attending the University of South Carolina with her cousin Miriam Robin. Miriam had lost a cap on a front tooth, which upset and embarrassed her, but there were few dentists available in Columbia because most had been drafted into the service. The Bass family, however, had an excellent dentist in North, Dr. Legare Davis. As Ruth explained the situation to her father, the operator interrupted, saying "Mr. Bass, do you want me to call Dr. Legare?" (In the South, it was considered polite to refer to someone by their title and first name, but it was always "Mr. Bass"—not "Mr. Nathan" —a subtle appellation that combined respect with a hint of distance rather than familiarity.)

The Bass girls were also fortunate that their family could afford domestic help, especially with Esther working most days in the store. They usually had a maid in the house, and were certainly lucky that they needed only to watch—rather than help—as their washwoman for many years built a fire weekly under a large iron pot into which she stirred their clothes in Octagon soap, or sometimes lye, to get them clean. Frances recalled that one of their maids, named Hannah, made a dish for the kids called "chow-chow pickle," so they called her "Hannah Chow-Chow Pickle." Jack's earliest memory "is sitting in a stroller under a pecan tree in the back yard, tended by a black woman."

By today's standards, the Bass family home in North was quite modest, but in the distressed economic environment of the 1930's, the Bass children must surely have felt part of the privileged class in their little community.

VIII. Practical Judaism In The Small Town South

As the only Jewish family in an isolated town filled with Protestant Christians, it must have been a challenge for Nathan and Esther to raise their children in Jewish tradition and culture. Nevertheless, they did their best.

Part of that process was simply keeping up with events around the world, which Nathan did by avidly reading his magazine subscriptions to *LIFE*, *Time,* and *Reader's Digest* from cover to cover when they arrived in the mail. He also read three local newspapers daily—*The State* and the *Columbia Record* from the capital city, and the *Times and Democrat* from the county seat of Orangeburg. To keep up with Jewish news and world events, Nathan also read the socialist *Der Tag* (The Day), a Yiddish language newspaper delivered in the mail.

Nathan's youngest son, Jack, who went on to become a journalist and Southern historian, later said of Nathan, "in the one-party Democratic South of that time, Daddy could safely express himself as a staunch advocate of Franklin D. Roosevelt and the New Deal. That nobody in town could read the newspaper [Der Tag] that most shaped his political views served him well."

Later, the Bass family also subscribed to a North Carolina publication called the *Carolina Israelite*, edited in Charlotte, N.C. by Harry Golden, who once wrote a short essay titled "The Town's Lone Jew." As if describing Nathan, Golden wrote:

> When he opens the store in the morning he may not know it, but the folks automatically identify him with Jeremiah, Isaiah, Amos, and the Second Coming, and all of this imposes a tremendous obligation on our "lone Jew" in a small southern town.

Nathan also stayed close to his sister Ida by corresponding with her every week, in Yiddish. He was a regular letter writer, keeping in touch with friends and relatives around the country.

Yet another source of news was the network of Jewish merchants in the small towns of the South. As Nathan's son Jack put it:

> In the mass migration of Jews from eastern Europe that began in the late nineteenth century, only a few came into such Southern ports as Charleston, Savannah, Mobile, New Orleans, and Galveston. But throughout the South in the first half of the 20th century, however, most of the towns the size of North had a Jewish family, almost invariably a merchant who through friends or relatives had some connection to the New York garment industry.
>
> Traveling salesmen served as a grapevine that provided news of Jewish families in neighboring towns— who was sick or prospering or traveling or sending sons or daughters to college. Daddy often invited the traveling salesmen home to dinner, the mid-day meal. They provided another window to the larger world.[41]

While Nathan and Esther tried to instill their children with Jewish teaching at home, it took the prompting of the local Baptist preacher to get them to seek a more formal Jewish education for their family. On a hot evening in 1935, North's Southern Baptist minister knocked on the door. "Mr. Bass," he said, "you have seven children and there is no Sunday school for Hebrew people in our little town."

"That's true, Reverend," said Nathan. "The closest Jewish community is in Columbia."

"Columbia! Why I reckon that's a long 30-mile drive. Why don't you bring your children to us? We're right here!"

The following Sunday morning, Nathan started up his 1930 Model A Ford as all the children but one year old Jack piled into the car. At the

---

41 Jack Bass, "Just Like One of Us," Unpublished research project for independent study at Emory University with Prof. Allan Tullos, at 23-24..

top speed of 30 mph, it took a full hour to reach the doors of Columbia's Reform Hebrew Tree of Life Temple[42], where the Bass children began their more formal religious education.[43]

The Sunday trips to Columbia developed into a family ritual that lasted until Lucille's confirmation. Jack remembers the five youngest children crowded into a 1939 Chevrolet sedan for the hour-long drive from North to Columbia. The kids played cow poker or four-legged animals, games in which they had teams that counted animals on the side of the road on which they were seated. They also played ABC's, a game in which teams competed to get all the letters of the alphabet sequentially from billboards on their side of the road. Everyone always looked for the sign advertising Quaker State Motor Oil when their team was up to the letter "Q". If anyone needed to go to the bathroom, Nathan would stop the car and the needy party would commune with nature behind a tree.

While waiting for the children to get out of religious school, Nathan would regularly stop by Rubin's Wholesale in Columbia, which was open on Sunday's. Hyman Rubin, who began work in the family store in 1935 after graduating from the University of South Carolina, reminisced that Nathan was "a delightful personality" who had "seven smart children."[44] After getting out of religious school, Sunday mornings also included a visit to Zussman's Bakery in Columbia to buy fresh-baked rye and pumpernickel bread and twist rolls, which may have reminded Nathan of his own mother's bakery in Vasiloshok. The family also stopped at "Groucho" Miller's delicatessen in Columbia for corned beef, lox, cream cheese, salt herring, sour cream, and matzo meal. Esther made blintzes, crisp potato latkes served with applesauce, gefilte fish from fresh shad bought on Assembly Street in Columbia, borscht and chopped liver that she served on saltine crackers. The Basses definitely were the only family in North whose grits were often mixed with fried salt herring that had

---

42 Unlike the Orthodox (now Conservative) Hebrew Beth Shalom synagogue, with which Nathan was already affiliated, the Tree of Life Temple had a Sunday religious school, which was the only time Nathan could bring his family to Columbia.

43 This account is taken from "Diamonds in the Sand," Jewish Press online, http://www.jewishpress.com/pageroute.do/32816/ (accessed 12/19/10), by Tzvi Jacobs, one of Nathan's grandsons. The story was related to Tzvi by his mother Ruth Bass Jacobs, who made the trip to Columbia many times.

44 See Rubin's Reminiscences, June 1993.

soaked overnight in a pan of fresh water, a meal the children regarded as a delicacy.

On the drive home from Sunday school, the Bass family would some-times stop and visit with another Jewish family, the Schechters, who lived in Swansea, a small town between North and Columbia. The Schechters had a nicely decorated home, and Lucille recalled her mother warning her not to touch Mrs. Schechter's "Balloon Lady" and "Balloon Man" figurines.

Sunday afternoons were also a time for socializing with other Jews. Often, the Stotsky family from Saluda and the Shapiros from Wagner would come over to play poker with Nathan. Lucille would watch, and when older, sometimes play, which no doubt was the source of her life-long success as a gambler. Other times, the Bass family would drive to Saluda, where the Stotskys ran what was known back then as a "five and dime"—a store where most products cost a nickel or a dime. The Bass children liked it when Gussie Stotsky, or her husband Nathan—who the Basses just called "Stotsky"—would take them down to the store and let them pick something out. One day, Gussie showed up in North in a brand new full length mink coat, which Nathan Bass praised although he probably thought it was quite an extravagance.

Nathan knew and maintained friendly relations with the Baptist and Methodist ministers—the two major white churches in North[45]—as well as the African-American preachers, most of whom also held other jobs. Indeed, the local clergymen would cite Nathan by name in exhorting their congregants to show more diligence in church attendance, point-ing out that Mr. Bass drove his children every week 30 miles each way to and from Columbia for Sunday School.

Because clergy were more esteemed and respected in the South, rabbis often found service in southern synagogues and temples more fulfilling. "The Southern atmosphere is pleasant for a rabbi; they are respected, are called 'doctor,' and many of them stay for long periods of time. 'Professionally,' said a Conservative rabbi, 'it's a nicer life here. It's the Bible belt, and the clergy has a higher standing. People in the South are less urbane and sophisticated, it's true, but they take religion a lot more seriously.'"[46]

---

45 There was also a small Pentecostal church in town.
46 Evans, *The Provincials*, at 94.

Overt anti-Semitism was rare, but on occasion an incident would occur that would highlight the Bass family's special status in the town. Once, when Frances was in the third grade, around Easter time, she came home from school and told her mother that her teacher said the Jews killed Jesus. Nathan and Esther were quite upset, although Frances couldn't understand why. Nathan went to see the school superintendent, who called in the teacher and straightened things out to Nathan's satisfaction. When Jack was in sixth grade, he got into a fight with another boy at recess, after an exchange of words. After Jack returned the boy's punch, knocking him to the ground, the boy cowered and blurted out "you ol' Jew." Jack walked away. It was the only anti-Semitic incident he remembered experiencing in 12 years of public school.

That's not to say that Southerners didn't harbor anti-Semitism. As Eli Evans points out in *The Provincials*, surveys of Southerners typically showed higher levels of anti-Jewish sentiment than in other regions of the country. Evans speculates that a significant part of that anti-Semitism, however, was a bias against all Yankees, and hence aimed more at the stereotype of "New York Jews."[47] It was also the case that Southern norms of politeness would discourage overt anti-Semitism of a personal sort, although anti-Jewish attitudes might still persist. Illustrative of the point, Jack recalls an incident once when he walked into a small grocery store near his father's store and heard a relative of the owner talking to others, around a pot belly stove, about "damned New York Jews." The man stopped with his story, however, as soon as Jack's presence was noticed.

It was certainly true that the Bass family rarely faced direct anti-Semitism of the sort that would have been common in the Jewish pale of the old country. Nonetheless, to some townfolk, the Bass family stood out as different. When the Bass sisters would go walking through town together, one man would see them and say, "Here comes the Jew girls." Yet the sisters really didn't think much of it. Just as Marcia didn't think twice about singing "The Lord's Prayer" with the school glee club when it made a special trip to Columbia to be on the radio. When Jack was a Boy Scout, however, he attended a couple of Baptist church services (the scoutmaster was also the preacher) and "found myself uncomfortable with the emotional intensity and emphasis on salvation through Jesus."

---

47 See Evans, *The Provincials*, at 190.

More often than not, however, the Bass family's Judaism was a source of curiosity to the rest of the town. Ruth recalls that one town tradition was a large picnic on Good Friday each Spring, which often coincided with Passover. The Bass children would attend the picnic with their friends, but if it was Passover, Esther would give them matzo—the flat unleavened bread traditional to the Jewish holiday—instead of bread. Esther quickly learned that she should pack extra matzo for such occasions, because the other children at the picnic, intrigued by the large square crackers, would want to have a taste of it.

Religious holidays were also special occasions for the Bass family. Each year on the high holy days of Rosh Hashanah and Yom Kippur, Nathan and Esther would drive the older children to Columbia for services, staying at the Jefferson Hotel, two blocks from Beth Shalom (House of Peace) Synagogue. Ruth recalls staying in the hotel as "the highlight of our year." It was "the first time we saw an elevator, and we loved riding up and down in it." In the orthodox Jewish tradition, the family could easily walk from the hotel to the synagogue for services, rather than drive.

The House of Peace Synagogue was here from 1910-1936.

The family would also go into the city for Simchas Torah, the Jewish holiday that marks completion of the annual cycle of reading of the Torah in synagogue. Sometimes, on the drive, Esther would regale the children with stories of growing up in New York and how observant they were, building a succah for the Fall holiday of Succos, taking shaloch manos to neighbors (i.e., delivering treats on the spring holiday of Purim) and strictly observing Shabbos (Sabbath). Esther also told the children of their father's cheder education at the Jewish school in Grodno.

On Chanukah, which occurs in December around the time of Christmas, the children lit candles each night and received Chanukah gelt—a nickel, dime or at most a quarter—from their parents. Christmas in North was a major holiday that effected a sufficiently strong cultural force that the Bass family would hang goodie-filled stockings by the fireplace when the kids were young. "More than any other time," said Jack, "Christmas day made me feel different, a feeling of being left out. As a boy, I learned to avoid visiting friends, who enthusiastically showed off their presents and found it natural to ask what I had gotten for Christmas."

Passover, in the Spring, was also a major holiday in the Bass household. On the first two nights of Passover the family held a Seder—the ritual dinner that memorializes the Jewish passage from slavery in Egypt. Marcia remembers her father reading in Hebrew from the family Haggadah—the special prayer book used to conduct the Passover meal. Cousins Nathan and Gussie Stotsky, before moving from Saluda to more distant Greenville, S.C., were almost always over for at least one of the Passover seders, as well as for Chanukah celebrations and Thanksgiving dinner.[48] The biblical injunction to take in the stranger on Passover was also honored and taken quite literally in the Bass household. Any Jews passing through North joined the family Seder. As the children grew older, they frequently brought home friends from college. Jack recalls once driving home to North from college with an entire carload of his fraternity brothers from Phi Epsilon Pi, a Jewish fraternity, for the Seder.

---

48 Estelle Lury, whose mother, Ida Stotsky Diatkin, was Nathan Bass's first cousin, recalls visits from Laurens, near Greenville, to North for Thanksgiving.

Although the Bass family did not keep kosher, they avoided pork and shellfish, and in the kosher tradition did not mix meat with dairy products in the same meal. Indeed, Esther would not use soap for washing dishes—instead using boiling water—because the soap of the time contained tallow, or pig fat. That wasn't enough for Esther's mother Rose, however, who brought her own set of kosher pots, pans and dishes in the early years in which she visited North. Rose was not able to visit later—Jack saw this grandmother of his only once, when he was 12 and accompanied Esther to see her aging mother at a retirement home on Long Island.

Nathan's fellow townsmen knew he didn't eat pork, so they accommodated him. When the Masons had ham at their regular dinners, they served Nathan chicken instead.

In 1931, the family had a very special occasion as the oldest boy, Bernie, turned 13. Studying with Rabbi David Karesh in Columbia, Bernie had his bar mitzvah, including a reception in North that "was talked about for many years" after by dozens of Jewish people from Columbia and elsewhere who drove in for the event. Bernie's next youngest sibling, Herbie, was a rebellious teenager who refused to have a bar mitzvah, and later in life acknowledged he wasn't very religious. At the time, it was not common for girls to have bat mitzvahs, and none of the Bass girls had one. The girls, however, were all confirmed at the reform Tree of Life Temple in Columbia.

When Jack turned 13, however, he had a bar mitzvah "of sorts." It was nothing like Bernie's. Jack, who had never attended a bar mitzvah before, was poorly prepared as a much older Nathan didn't involve himself in the training and their rabbi had grown quite old. With the aged rabbi leading him in stage whispers, Jack stumbled through the Hebrew while a dozen or so of Nathan's friends stood around talking. Afterwards, they opened a bottle of whiskey and toasted him. Years later, Jack said he had decided "the important thing about my bar mitzvah was that I had it, that it was a rite of passage in which I participated."[49]

---

49 Because of his experience, Jack made sure his children attended bar or bat mitzvahs before their own, and saw to it that they were properly trained, notwithstanding that he was of little help because he'd never mastered the full Hebrew alphabet. When his oldest son, Ken, was bar mitzvahed, Jack was quite proud that his orthodox Jewish brother-in-law pronounced it a "flawless" performance. Jack also had the occasion to pass the Torah to two of his grandsons in their bar mitzvah ceremonies.

It wasn't that Nathan wanted to ignore Jack's Jewish training. Jewish education, which had been so crucial in Nathan's own upbringing, including his years in the cheder school in Grodno, was important to the family. When Jack was older, Nathan wanted to send him to Yeshiva—a prospect Jack wasn't too happy about—but Jack's limited Jewish training in the reform Sunday School hardly qualified him and so he wasn't admitted.

Nathan also observed his mother and father's yahrtzeits—a ceremonial remembrance on the anniversary of a parent's death—by reciting Kaddish (the Jewish prayer for mourning) and turning on a closet light off the kitchen for 24 hours from sunset to sunset.

Ruth Bass, who later married an orthodox Jew from Charleston and maintained a strictly kosher home, recalled that her father Nathan "exemplified all that is positive in Judaism. We never heard the words tzedekah (charity) or hachness orchim (hospitality, welcoming guests), but we saw these concepts practiced—as well as honesty in personal and business dealings, brotherhood of man, love of family, patriotism—practiced every day. The lessons Daddy learned in cheder stayed with him throughout his life." Esther, too, practiced Jewish customs of charity and friendship to strangers, and joined Hadassah, the Jewish women's Zionist organization, in Columbia.

Nathan never achieved wealth, but his life can hardly be viewed as anything other than a success. Except for overindulgence in smoking, he generally practiced moderation. He seldom used a swear word, and it took considerable provocation to cause him to lose his temper. He didn't consume mixed drinks, but he normally imbibed a small amount, less than a shot glass, of whiskey daily.

Nathan was also known as a soft touch for "schnorrers." Harry Golden wrote, "Literally, schnorrer means, 'beggar.' But, historically, the schnorrer was a beloved wanderer among Jewish communities... The American schnorrer is another story, of course." At the dog tracks and nightclubs of Miami, Golden wrote, "The word is out ... Schnorrers—stay clear of Columbia, South Carolina, on your way back to New York next season" because "they decided to give each schnorrer, regardless of his story or gimmick, the sum of one dollar—no questions asked."

When a beggar stopped by the store during the Depression, Esther would tell Nathan not to give them any money. Instead, if they were hungry, he was to send them to the house, down the road, where Esther would serve them a meal. In many instances, however, the schnorrer got both—a dollar and a meal. The children thought the rabbi in Columbia steered them to North, or perhaps that word got out on the Schnorrer grapevine—skip Columbia and stop in North!

Exemplifying the Jewish tradition of tzedakah, whenever a solicitation would come in the mail for money, Nathan would send them a dollar, which added up to several hundred dollars a year by the late 1940's when his annual net income was less than $5,000. His daughter Marcia does the same thing today.

Esther and Nathan complemented each other, forming a true partnership in their marriage. When they wanted to talk privately, it was in Yiddish. The children never learned to speak more than a few words of the old world language because the message conveyed to them was that they weren't supposed to learn it. Occasionally, however, a little Yiddish came in handy for the children—for example, while working in the store, the children would use the Yiddish term "ganiff," which means thief, if they saw someone stealing, after which Nathan would handle the matter. But, that was an exception. While instilling Jewish values in their children, Nathan and Esther, like many immigrants, wanted their children to grow up thoroughly American. That desire, and their patriotism, would later lead to the ultimate sacrifice, when their second eldest son eagerly signed up for the Marine Corps as World War II loomed.

IX. Social Life In North

Although the Bass family maintained its Jewish identity, the children were largely assimilated into the social life of a small southern town. In many ways, the children would have been difficult for an outsider to distinguish from their white protestant neighbors.

Life in North had its pleasures, and in many ways the Bass family was just as typical as any other in town. In the 1930's, before the first movie theater came to North, tent shows were the big attraction. The promoter would erect a huge tent in the center of town to show free movies, mostly silent films. The catch was that, while changing reels on the movies, the promoter would sell patent medicines to the assembled throng. These medicines, at least 50 percent (100 proof) alcohol, were supposed to cure any ailment. The traveling tent show made a killing because everyone had something wrong with themselves and if nothing else the alcoholic "medicine" made everyone—especially the teetotalling Baptists and Methodists—feel good, at least for awhile.

When the children were a bit older, North got its first movie house, which showed westerns on Saturdays and held a jackpot drawing for a set of dishes on Wednesday nights. Jack recalled going to the New Theater, as it was called, with his sister Lucille, and watching three showings of westerns on Saturdays, usually Roy Rogers, Gene Autry, Johnny Mack Brown, Tex Ritter or Hopalong Cassidy.[50] When "Gone With The Wind" came to town, the Mayor treated the entire school (presumably the white school only) to a showing. The movie theater didn't last long, however—it was closed by the time Marcia was in high school, such that her senior class trip in 1944 went to Columbia where she saw Tyrone Power in the movie "Johnny Apollo."

For relatives and friends, who frequently came through to visit, the town was an enigma. Once, Nathan was showing some Yankee relatives

---

50 Cassidy's real name was William Boyd. Jack met him years later at a restaurant near Encenada, Mexico, while in the Navy and stationed near San Diego.

the sights of North. They drove by the two-cell jail, the schoolhouses (a brick one for whites and a wooden one for blacks), the cotton platform in the middle of downtown loaded with bales of cotton to be shipped out by Seaboard Railway, and finally the cotton gin that removed the cotton seed and packed the freshly picked cotton lint into 500 pound bales. One cousin remarked, "I didn't know they made gin from cotton!"

Another time, the family took some cousins from California to the North Hotel for Sunday dinner. One cousin, disdaining the ubiquitous iced tea, asked the waitress for soda. To his surprise, the waitress came out carrying a tray with a glass of water and a box of Arm and Hammer baking soda—in North the only term designating a carbonated beverage was a "soft drink."

Friends of Esther's sister, Fanny, once made a side trip to North on their way home from Florida, after promising Fanny they would go and meet her sibling. Nathan, of course, invited them over to the house for dinner. When they returned to New York, they told Fanny they were shocked that her sister and husband couldn't afford to buy shoes for all their children, unaware that during the hot summer months it was customary for most children in the rural South to go barefoot, both inside the house and outside.[51]

For the Bass family, having relatives in other parts of the country gave the children unique opportunities to travel and be exposed to new ideas, unlike most of their friends in town. In 1939, for example, when Ruth was a junior in high school, she and Frances went to New York City to see the World's Fair, staying with their grandma Rose and Aunt Fanny in Brooklyn. On the same trip they stopped in South River, New Jersey to see their Aunt Ida and spend time with their cousins Miriam and Esther, who were about the same age.

Lucille had a big trip of her own. Nathan Stotsky's brother, Morris, who lived in Lancaster, Pennsylvania, had come to visit North with his son Max.[52] While at the Bass home, the Stotskys invited 11-year-old

---

51 Fanny lived in Brooklyn most of her life. She married Harry Slomin and had four sons, who the Basses in North knew as Robbie, Manny, Jerry and Eddie. Robbie's son Michael, a lawyer in New Jersey, has remained in close contact with Marcia Bass Brody over the years.

52 The Stotskys' mother was Nathan Bass's aunt (she was Schmuel Bass's sister). Hence Nathan was first cousins with Morris Stotsky, Nathan Stotsky and their sister Ida Diatkin.

Lucille to go back to Pennsylvania and visit with them for awhile.[53] On her trip to Lancaster, Lucille also stayed with some other cousins, the Solomons and Silvers. Lucille then took a train to New Jersey, where her Aunt Ida met her. She also visited New York, where her Aunt Sadye acted as tour guide, taking Lucille to see the Statue of Liberty and the Empire State Building.[54] After an enjoyable trip up north, Lucille met her father in New York, returning home with him by train.

Even within the state of South Carolina, the Basses traveled more than most, with their frequent trips to Columbia, to Saluda to visit the Stotsky family and occasionally to Charleston for visits to local Jewish wholesalers there. During the summer, the family would drive to Sesquicentennial State Park, near Columbia, for swimming and picnics.

Of course, the children also interacted with various aunts, uncles, cousins and other relatives who would visit North. Estelle Lury recalled spending a week in North when she was 15. "I felt like it was a home away from home because I was treated like one of the family. I had never been on a bicycle, and during that week I was taught to ride one. I

Ida's daughter, Estelle, would visit South Carolina often, and eventually met and married Meyer Lury from Laurens, S.C., where she settled. Her son Mark Lury grew up in Laurens and, with his mother, was often a part of Bass family gatherings in the state.

53 While Max Stotsky's father was in North, Lucille witnessed him putting on tefillin. Tefillin are two specially designed leather boxes containing parchments, on which are written certain Biblical passages. There are leather straps going through them so they can be secured to the head and the arm. There is one for the head and a different one for the arm. Jewish men put these on weekday mornings in fulfillment of the Biblical command (Deuteronomy 11:18) to "...bind them for a sign on your arm, and let them be an insignia in the center of your head...". Lucille ran in the bedroom and told Mama she thought something was wrong with him. Esther told her daughter there was nothing wrong—it was just a special way to pray.

54 Esther's sister Sadye married late in life and had no children. She lived in Washington, D.C. for many years, helping her husband run a shop on Fourteenth St., then moved to California. After her husband died, Sadye moved to Columbia, S.C. to be near her nieces and nephews from South Carolina. Esther also had a brother, Jack, who lived in the Bronx and worked in a bank. Jack had no children. When Jack Bass at 12 visited New York, his Uncle Jack took him to the Polo Grounds, where they watched baseball legend Mel Ott play one of his final games for the New York Giants. Slomin cousins took him to a Brooklyn Dodgers game at Ebbetts Fields, and his mother took him to see the Rockettes at Radio City Music Hall and to the Hayden Planetarium.

also remember going swimming in a swimming hole—it wasn't a pool." Later, after her marriage and move to Laurens, Estelle also visited North many times for Thanksgiving, recalling "there was always a full house at the Bass home in North." Once, when her newborn son Mark was only three months old, she had left behind the bag she had with diapers, formula and bottles. Nathan quickly calmed her down, drove into town, and purchased the necessary items for her baby.

Estelle Lury and her son Mark.

Another frequent visitor was Marilyn Cohn, whose father, David E. Cohn, was Esther's brother. Marilyn was born in South Carolina, but did most of her growing up in Washington, D.C.[55] "Although we loved Washington, most of my summer and holiday vacations were spent visiting family back in South Carolina," primarily in St. Matthews, which was the

---

55 David Cohn worked for many years for the Federal Bureau of the Budget (known today as the Office of Management and Budget). Marilyn married Arnold Fine, who had a public relations firm in Washington. Marilyn worked for some time at the Department of Housing and Urban Development (HUD).

hometown of Marilyn's mother, Janet Pearlstine. Marilyn was an only child, so she really enjoyed the frequent visits to North, where she had seven cousins (she also had cousins, on the other side of her family, in St. Matthews and Charleston). "Our trips to North were usually for several hours, with a visit to the Bass home, frequently a mid-day or evening meal, playing with my cousins and always a visit to the Bass store. The store visit was a special treat because I knew that my uncle or aunt would always suggest that I pick something out for a present to take home. I would be given lots of time to wander up and down the aisles to select 'the perfect gift.'"

Nathan was a gregarious sort for whom North's social life was important. Despite his Yiddish accent, prematurely gray hair and small frame, Nathan managed to earn the admiration and respect of the other men in town. He regularly attended meetings of the Masonic Lodge in North, as well as Wednesday afternoon "fish fries" with many of those lodge brothers. The merchants all closed their stores at noon on Wednesday. It turned out those "fish fries" were community poker games, which allowed Nathan to engage in his favorite form of recreation—penny, nickel and dime poker (as well as eat fried fish). Nathan had the ability to get along with people—he respected others and earned their respect in return.

Nathan also felt a responsibility to his community. Improvement of the lot of the small farmer was of definite concern to him. On his annual buying trips to New York, Nathan would note the scarcity and relatively high prices of fresh foods that were readily available in South Carolina. After contacting a few food wholesalers, he came home and got the farmers interested in raising the crops for sale out of state. In this manner, he helped organize the first shipment of sweet potatoes from South Carolina to northern markets. This was in the middle of the Depression, when sweet potatoes had, for awhile, become an important cash crop for South Carolina farmers.

Nathan also dabbled for a while in tomatoes, shipping crates of them north in a partnership with North businessman Clarence Culler long before that crop became the success it is today in South Carolina. Neither venture proved personally profitable, but a subsequent mayor of North later stated that Nathan's "efforts in promoting a farmers marketplace here and encouraging farmers to plant vegetables and other side crops other than corn and cotton," along with other "community improvements," had helped the people of the town to "have a better way of life."[56]

Nathan Bass and Clarence Culler show off their tomatoes. Zack Culler is in the background.

Nathan also did his best to rise above the petty and often mean-spirited racial politics of the South. The term "nigger" was never uttered, and would not have been tolerated, in the Bass household. Blacks in South Carolina at the time were second-class citizens, subjected to official discrimination and segregation that had been upheld dec-ades earlier by the U.S. Supreme Court. Nathan, however, operated his store on a one-price cash basis, welcoming all customers regardless of

---

56 Letter dated July 26, 1986 from M.E. Livingston to Ruth Jacobs.

race. Nathan didn't discriminate, either, on the rare occasions when he granted credit to a customer, such as Burley Oliver, an African-American yeoman farmer who, in outfitting his entire family of many children at Bass Mercantile, became a preferred customer. Oliver grew cotton on his own land, earning Nathan's trust and paying his bills when the crop was harvested and sold. Nathan also extended credit to M.E. "Mutt" Livingston, who later became Mayor of North, when he was in high school, for "a badly needed pair of pants to wear to school."[57]

Nathan was familiar with discrimination from his days living in the Russian Pale. He was also familiar with biblical injunctions on justice and the treatment of strangers, including the admonition that Jews should remember their forced servitude in Egypt in deciding how to relate to others. Nathan was not unique in this regard. As Eli Evans describes, "[d]uring Reconstruction, the Jew as peddler and the black man as freedman found each other out of economic necessity; and once the thousands of East European immigrants made the transition from peddler to shopkeeper, the black man moved with him to the only store in town that extended credit, addressed him and his wife as 'Mr.' and 'Mrs.,' and allowed his family to try on clothes before buying them. Though the black man was as fundamentalist in his religious beliefs as his white neighbors, part of his soul lay with the Israelites of the Old Testament, and so religious anti-Semitism was never a central part of his emotions."[58]

The role of women in the South at the time was generally more circumscribed. Most women, especially in rural areas, worked at home, raising their families. Socially, they would be most active in their churches. For this reason, Esther was less actively involved in the community socially, but she joined the PTA, the local bridge club, and was always a fixture in the store. One neighbor later recalled seeing Esther "passing our house on the way to the store every morning about 9 or 9:30."[59] In later years, Jack would drive her to Columbia to make social visits with some of her Jewish women friends there.

---

57 Id.
58 Evans, The Provincials, at 272-73.
59 Letter dated July 26, 1986 from M.E. Livingston to Ruth Jacobs.

For the children, social life in the small town of North seemed fairly normal, although they were sometimes reminded that they were different. Ruth, the oldest daughter, recalled that much of social life in the community revolved around the church. When she was older, her classmates would tell her every Monday of the exciting things that had happened in church the day and night before—in the choir, or youth group, or Sunday school—and she would feel left out.

But the Bass children rarely, if ever, felt ostracized or isolated. Ruth would play with her neighbor, Annie "Bruce" Livingston, "every afternoon," frequently heading to the drug store downtown for a Coke or ice cream. A Coke cost six cents, and the two girls would ask for an extra glass so they could share one. Marcia was good friends with next door neighbor Thelma Livingston, along with classmate Eliza Day—who she still exchanges holiday greetings with—and Betty Jean Livingston. Marcia would ask her father for a penny or a nickel—which he always obliged. She could "buy five silver bells" for a penny, and "a nickel would buy you an ice cream cone." When she got ice cream, Marcia "would bite the bottom of the cone and suck the ice cream through it—so messy and so good!"

Frances and her two friends, Betty Culler and Jean Lybrand, made up a threesome--when you saw one you always saw the other two. They would take turns eating at each other's houses. Jean moved away when Frances was in the fifth grade, but Betty and Frances remained friends through the years.

Lucille's best friend for years was Pat Johnson, who would come to town to stay with her grandparents. They would play in Pat's grandfather's warehouse. She was also friends with Rose Reed at school, but because Rose lived "in the country" they rarely saw each other outside school. Later, when the Blaine family moved in across the street, Lucille would visit her girlfriend Jackie and feast on peanut butter crackers.

Jack had good friends growing up, including first cousins Eddie and John William Reed,[60] cousins Jimmy and Joseph Whetstone, Otis Jones, next door neighbor Shirley Livingston, and later Buddy Frick. As a preschooler, Jack had "the run of the town." As he got older, he went hunting and fishing with Eddie Reed, "enough to appreciate the outdoors."

---

60 Nathan and Esther lived with their grandparents for a time shortly after they were married.

The children rarely had birthday parties, however, perhaps because of what happened when their mother had one for Frances. Marcia recalled "everyone getting wild and knocking down a cabinet of dishes in the kitchen."

For the most part, the Bass children enjoyed life. One cherished activity was listening to the radio. Marcia liked "Lux Radio Theater," "Lights Out," and "Fibber Magee and Molly." Lucille was a "Lone Ranger" fan, while Ruth couldn't wait for the daily edition of "Little Orphan Annie," sponsored by Ovaltine. Ruth was thrilled when the secret metal decoder she'd ordered from the radio arrived in the mail, allowing her to decode messages read during the show. The whole family listened to comedy shows such as Amos and Andy, Jack Benny, and Fred Allen, and Nathan never missed catching the 11 pm news. Nathan was a good storyteller in his own right, as well, usually telling the four girls a different story each night before they went to bed.

The girls had their own games, too. One was "Lucille, Marcia, Frances, Mine," which Ruth recalls playing with the Butler Brothers catalogue, which was similar to Sears. Each sister would take a page, select one or two items from it and tell a story of what they'd do with it.

On other days, the children might just go down to the railroad depot and watch trains come through, or go with friends to the swimming holes at Midway or Poole's Mill (the latter of which extended out more than six feet deep). Jack would later ride out with friends whose fathers drove them to a swimming hole at Jerusalem Creek, several miles out of town. If it was spring or early summer, they'd eat red plums right off the bushes on their way to the swimming hole. That time of year they also helped tend a garden on the plot of land behind the back yard. In the Fall, Marcia recalled playing touch football in front of the Methodist Church. The girls would also roller skate on the sidewalk in front of their house (one of the few sidewalks in North), or take a special trip to the roller rink in nearby Denmark.

The children learned from each other, and from their friends. As Marcia put it: "No one took swimming lessons. No one took bicycle lessons. No one took driving lessons. No one took bridge lessons. We just learned." An exception was music—Lucille "can still see and hear

Frances in the living room playing the violin while we stayed on the front porch watching through the window."

Card games were also a major source of entertainment for the whole Bass family. Everyone learned to play bridge, and Nathan kept a stash of poker chips. One day, the local Southern Baptist preacher visited the house and asked preschooler Jack if he could count. Jack said yes, and proceeded to count off "1, 2, 3 ... 9, 10, Jack, Queen, King, Ace." Whether the preacher was horrified—Baptists were against playing cards—or simply quietly amused, no one could be sure, as he didn't say anything.

The children had a number of pets, including a cat named Betty and a dog named Friskie. The dog earned the girls' enmity when, at a time when nylon was rationed, she grabbed all the freshly washed nylon hose from the clothesline and chewed them up.

Bernie, who was the consummate "big brother" to the girls, would bring them gifts, serve as their protector, and share his wisdom. Frances recalls once when she sat with Bernie on the front porch swing during one of South Carolina's classic summer thunderstorms, telling her the lightning was "like moving pictures in the sky." With Marcia, Bernie sat in the back yard at night pointing out different constellations. He would sing Marcia to sleep with "Sweet and Low," notwithstanding that he, like most of the Bass children, couldn't really carry a tune.

The youngest child, Jackie, was "the pet of the family" according to Ruth. She would swing him to sleep on the front porch swing, and Bernie would sing Brahms's lullaby to him. While home from college, Bernie especially spent many hours playing with Jackie, teaching him to catch and throw balls and play sports. With summers at ROTC camp, Herbie was home far less often.

Another summer treat was homemade ice cream, sometimes served with fresh watermelon. Marcia and Lucille, as the smallest of the girls, would take turns sitting on the ice cream churn so it wouldn't move while the others turned the crank.

Socializing with other children in town also meant eating at each other's homes. Esther was not known as a particularly good cook, but the children loved her chop suey and chicken salad. She also specialized in "icebox cookies"—called that because Esther refrigerated the rolls of cookie dough, which were filled with pecans, and simply cut out cookies when she needed them. Another dessert favorite was heavenly hash. On occasion Esther would make fresh squeezed orange juice.

Still, Marcia recalled looking forward to eating Sunday dinner—dinner being the midday meal in the small town South—at her friend Betty Jean's, where they always served fried chicken, rice and butter beans. Betty Jean, however, didn't quite as much look forward to eating at the Bass home. Served chopped liver on one occasion, she couldn't understand how her friend could possibly eat the stuff.

Jack frequently ate dinner at friends' homes. Although he never ate pork products or shellfish—both unkosher—at home, Jack ate whatever his friends ate when he visited them, and so developed a taste for pork chops that later in life manifested itself in a "penchant for roadside barbecue." He also learned to "enjoy the full range of traditional Southern food—fried chicken, fish, rice and gravy, biscuits, corn bread, turnip greens, butter (lima) beans, collards, rutabagas, corn on the cob, okra and tomatoes, pickled okra, chocolate cake or brownies for dessert," and sweetened iced tea to drink.

Jack recalls playing with friends climbing atop the cotton bales, or hiding in cracks of space between them, or later resting atop them after high school football practice while downing a "belly-washer"—a 12 ounce bottle of Pepsi-Cola, as distinguished from the more typical six-ounce Coke.

Like the second generation of most immigrant families to America, the Bass children were fairly well assimilated in absorbing the values and culture of their community.

X. Gettin' Educated

It was important to Nathan to educate his children, just as his parents had made sacrifices to make sure he had received good schooling. The options in North were limited, but adequate. There were two schools in town—one for whites and one for blacks. The Bass children attended a two-story brick building that initially housed eleven grades, from elementary through high school.[61] There was no kindergarten. The grammar school was downstairs, with the high school upstairs. In the early years, the school had no lights—only what nature provided through the large windows. By the time Jack enrolled in first grade in 1940, the elementary grades were housed in a separate brick building, attached to the original building by a covered walkway.

The "colored school," for black children, only went through grade nine. If an African-American student wanted to go to high school, he or she would have to travel 18 miles to Orangeburg, which few could afford. The black schools also opened a few weeks later than the white schools to allow sharecropper families to engage their children in handpicking the cotton crop.[62] Such was the state of education in the segregated South of the time.

At the white school, students stood in the lunch line in the school's kitchen with tin cups to receive a ladle of soup, along with a sandwich. The school had no gymnasium—just an outdoor basketball court. Once a year, the Orangeburg County Health Department would send

---

61 In 1948 a 12th grade was added as part of a statewide mandate (the year after Lucille graduated). As a result, Jack went through grade 12.

62 Black sharecroppers typically grew cotton on fields owned by white landowners, who supplied them with a small home and living necessities during the year in exchange for half (some took more) of the proceeds of the harvest when it came in. In addition to picking the cotton on the land they tilled, blacks worked as pickers for hire on land planted by whites. During the Depression years, a picker would earn as little as 50 cents per hundred pounds. A skilled adult picker could average 200 pounds per day, enough to earn one dollar. Blacks seldom earned enough to break out of the cycle of sharecropping.

someone to North to vaccinate the children. When the Bass children needed vaccinations, they went down to the cotton platform, in the middle of Main Street and parallel to the railroad tracks, where bales of cotton would sit before being sold and shipped to a mill by freight train. There, the town's children lined up for their shots, highlighting the expansive role of the cotton platform in the town's culture.[63]

The teachers in the white school were generally quite good. Graduates of North High School had gone on to many prominent positions within the state. Such was not the case for the black school, where some teachers had never attended college. One summer, Ruth Bass was working at the Post Office and saw a postcard mailed by one of the teachers from the black school. It made her ill to see that just about every word was misspelled. Some African-Americans in North nevertheless overcame this disadvantage—the black school principal's son, Lewis Dowdy, later became president of North Carolina A&T College, a historically black school. The obvious disparities between the white and the "colored" school would make an impact on the Bass children, especially Jack when he later covered, first hand as a journalist, some of the key moments in the Civil Rights revolution, and when he later wrote about the era in a series of books.

While the school curriculum focused on the "three R's," some of the electives reflected the issues of the day. For example, Marcia had to choose between French and a course described as "Man and the Motor Car."

Being in a small school in a small town had its advantages. Ruth, who described herself as a "klutz," was nonetheless able to be a substitute on the girls' basketball team. She was in the Glee Club notwithstanding that she "couldn't carry a tune." And she had a role in some of the school plays, such as the part of the French maid from Paris (Kentucky) in "Bashful Mr. Bobbs," where the romantic lead towered over her at six feet tall.

The Bass girls also had an advantage when it came to school plays—their mother had a pull-out closet in the store with "every kind of costume

---

63 Medical care was available, but limited. North had at least one physician and a dentist, but the children would go to see the latter only if they had a toothache. Marcia went once with a sore tooth and he pulled it without giving her any anesthesia. She says that's why she is, to this day, "literally scared to death of a dentist."

imaginable," as Lucille put it. Esther had saved every costume, whether it be from Halloween, a school play, or a little skit, that her children had worn from Bernie on down. Perhaps that's how Lucille landed the lead female role in her senior class play. Having parents who owned a store was also advantageous on Valentine's Day—Marcia and a friend would go to Bass Mercantile, pick out a large hatbox, and cut a hole in the box cover for all the valentines from the schoolchildren.

Marcia also played on the basketball team—while travelling with the team she saw her first indoor gymnasium. Marcia was a member of the Glee Club, the Beta Club and the business manager for the school newspaper. Like her older sister Ruth, Marcia tested her thespian talents in a couple of school plays. In one, she was supposed to kiss a boy wearing a fake mustache as a disguise, with the mustache going from his lips to hers, thereby revealing his true identity. Marcia was scared to death because she had never kissed a boy before. The same gregarious streak that made Marcia want to be in school plays, however, could cause trouble. In the sixth grade, Marcia frequently had to stay after school and write, 100 times, "I will not talk in school" (or, occasionally, stand in the corner of the classroom) for being too talkative with her classmates.

When Jack was in the third grade, he participated in schoolyard boxing matches refereed by the school principal. The boys used boxing gloves, and Jack recalls "getting knocked down three times in two matches and knocking down my opponent once." Later, Jack was an active participant in school sports, playing baseball, basketball and football in high school.

Jack Bass in football gear for North High School.

When Jack was in the seventh grade, the school superintend-ent learned that he knew how to score a baseball game, a skill Bernie had taught him. The superintendent, a first cousin of Brooklyn Dodg-ers pitcher Kirby Higby, was playing third base for the newly organized North Pirates, a semipro baseball team that played similar teams from other towns in the area. Initially, there were no night games because the fields were still not lighted. The superintendent arranged for Jack to be excused early from school to accompany the team to out-of-town games as its official scorer. While with the team, Jack interacted with men of all classes, ranging from the superintendent to sawmill workers and farmers—all white, of course, as it would have been inconceivable to have an integrated baseball team in South Carolina as that time. He rode in a car with four adult men, listening to them talk. "I wouldn't have learned nearly as much as early in life by staying for the final class period in the seventh grade," said Jack, "including a clear understanding that sports were intimately tied to the very definition of American manhood."

With all the grades in school together, the younger children some-times got opportunities that wouldn't exist elsewhere. In the sixth grade, Frances was asked by family friend Bruce Livingston, who was several years older, to participate in Bruce's class play, an experience that thrilled Frances and made her feel "grown up." Frances clearly enjoyed the limelight—another time she, along with her shy sister Ruth, deliv-ered a "commercial" for their daddy's store during a beauty contest by holding up a sign. They were supposed to say "Bass Mercantile Com-pany, Outfitters for the Entire Family," but Ruth got so nervous she for-got the words.

Then again, a small school could be stressful, too. The social high-light in high school was the Junior-Senior banquet, an elaborate affair planned over the course of the entire school year and North High's equivalent of a prom. Although it was not a dance—the local preachers frowned on that kind of thing—the girls wore formal gowns and had dates. Ruth, the oldest girl, was shy and no one asked her to the ban-quet. Her mother suggested trying some of her Sunday school class-mates from Columbia, but she was too reticent to ask. Instead, her big brother Bernie—then a law student—took Ruth to both her junior and senior years of the banquet.

In her senior year, Frances found herself in a tight race for valedicto-rian of her nine-member class with her best friend, Betty Culler. Frances edged out her friend, who later settled in Columbia as the wife of Rhett Jackson, who among other ventures owned the city's best bookstore, once served as president of the American Booksellers Association, and provided enlightened leadership as a Methodist layman during the tur-bulent desegregation era while serving as chairman of the state's Pro-bation, Pardon and Parole Board. The highlight of Lucille's senior year was the class trip, on a chartered bus, to Washington, D.C.—the class spent a good deal of the year working to raise the money for their tour.

When he was in high school, Jack was a good pitcher, going 21-4 over four years, but football was the sport he really enjoyed. He played both sports all four years of high school. "The school was small enough that if you could stand up straight and put on shoulder pads, you could make the team," he said of football. Jack missed only one game in four years. In his sophomore year, the big game against Swansea was scheduled for a Tuesday, instead of Thursday or Friday night like most other games. It was Yom Kippur, so he told the coach he couldn't play. "My parents didn't tell me I couldn't play. I just accepted it as a given."[64]

Jack was also politically aware while in school, and reflected his parents' more progressive views. In 1948, when Jack was in ninth grade, his civics teacher—who coached all the sports teams and subsequently went to law school and later served in the state legislature—conducted a secret ballot of the students in the coming presidential election. That year, South Carolina governor Strom Thurmond was running as an independent "states rights" candidate on a racially tinged platform against Democrat Harry Truman and Republican Thomas Dewey. After the vote, the teacher announced there were five votes for Thurmond and one—Jack's—for Truman. The teacher wasn't surprised.[65]

About the time the children started high school, they could also begin to drive a car: in those days one could get a license at age 14. A man from the State Highway Department would come around to North once a month to administer driving tests. No driver training courses existed in North, however, so the test could be quite a challenge. When Marcia reached her fourteenth birthday, she was eager to get her license. The first time she took the test, the man administering it asked her to read the letters on a chart. "What letters?" said Marcia. That's when she learned she needed eyeglasses. After getting glasses, Marcia returned to take the test again, but this time she couldn't see over the steering

---

64 Years later, Jack identified with Los Angeles Dodgers star pitcher Sandy Koufax, who sat out the opening game of the 1965 World Series because it was Yom Kippur.
65 Jack later co-authored an "unauthorized" biography of Thurmond. See Jack Bass and Marilyn Thompson, *Ol' Strom, An Unauthorized Biography of Strom Thurmond*, 1998 (Longstreet Press). They later co-authored *STROM: The Complicated Personal and Political Life of Strom Thurmond*, Public Affairs Press, 2003.

wheel because she was so small. So the man told her to bring a pillow for her next test, which she flunked because she didn't hold her hand out long enough to signal a turn. Finally, after several months of coming back, Marcia got her license.

For Lucille, the quest to drive was easier—she forgot to give any hand signals as she went through the driving test, then the patrolman who conducted the test asked her if she knew how to stop the car. Lucille claims he gave her the license "rather than having to take me out again." For Jack it took three tries.

For the seven Bass children in North, the public education provided at their school was sufficient, as we'll see later, for them all to go on to college and eventually function successfully in the adult world.

XI. Working The Store

A rite of passage for all the Bass children was working in their parents' store—Bass Mercantile Co. The store, roughly 50 feet wide and almost three times as deep, sold dry goods, meaning mostly clothes, household furnishings, toiletries and a variety of shoes (including the "Red Goose" brand). Back then, a lot of people sewed their own clothes, so a significant item was material sold by the yard. The big sales day in the store was Saturday in the fall—cotton-picking time and the peak season in the local economy. Farm families from the surrounding countryside would come into town to shop on those Saturdays. When the Bass children were old enough, they were expected to help out in the store, especially on Saturdays.

The cash register was located in the middle of the store. In the front was a radio, and in the back was the hand-cranked telephone and a stove for heat. Nathan and Esther employed extra clerks—all of them women—in the store on Saturdays, and it was the children's job initially to assist them. Lucille recalls working with Pearl and Ladenia Livingston, and Miss Leila Axson, who left a strand of pearls for Lucille when she passed away.

Jack started working in the store when he was seven. His first job was to deliver men's dress trousers to Maggie Reed, a seamstress who would sew the cuffs for men's trousers and make other alterations on her home sewing machine. Jack would ride his bike over to the Reed home with a heavy paper carrying bag hanging off his handle bars. He would then wait for "Miss Maggie" to finish, unless there were more than one pair of trousers to be cuffed, and then bring them back to the store five blocks away.

Another of Jack's early tasks was to take special orders from the store clerks for their Saturday evening meals. He would go to the Blue Moon Café and get them hot dogs or hamburgers, along with fries and a drink—Coke, Pepsi, Seven-Up or RC Cola. The Blue Moon was basically a "honky-tonk," the only place in North serving beer. Jack picked up quite a new vocabulary hanging around the Blue Moon, waiting for his order to be filled on Saturday evenings, when it was filled with a rough crowd of sharecroppers, tenant farmers, yeomen, and sawmill workers from the surrounding countryside (all white, of course), who used language a bit coarser than the "genteel town elite" of North.

N. BASS & CO.

THE HOME OF SATISFACTION

DRY GOODS, READY-TO-WEAR,
NOTIONS, *and* SHOES

We Are Delighted to Serve You at Any Time

OUR NEW QUARTERS ARE IN THE LEYSATH BUILDING
NEXT TO THE BANK OF NORTH.

Ad for Nathan's store in 1924 North High School Yearbook.

The store clerks were rarely allowed to attend the register. Instead, that was for Nathan and Esther, and for the older children on Saturdays. When Jack was in the eighth grade, his sister Lucille went off to college, giving Jack his first shot at operating the hand-cranked cash register, a job he'd been looking forward to for years. All of the children were paid for their work, giving them spending money during the week.

The children also sold merchandise of just about any kind—although Jack stayed away from lingerie. Jack enjoyed selling shoes. He was good at it. The secret for selling shoes to sharecropper and tenant farmer wives who worked in the fields, he figured out, "was to get a shoe that fit, no matter how big the foot, and tell the customer with conviction, 'that shoe *looks good* on your foot.'"

Dorothy Brown Wiseman, who later moved to Charleston, grew up in a large farm family—16 children—near North, and recalled that every pair of shoes she ever had until she was 15 years old came from Bass Mercantile Store. "You came in the store and the shoes were on the right. Mr. and Mrs. Bass always wanted to get for you what you wanted. They would lean over backwards to be sure you got what you wanted."[66] She recalled that the store was lined with shelves all the way to the ceiling, and that Mr. or Mrs. Bass would take a ladder around the shelves and climb up and get whatever someone needed.

Wiseman never knew that the Basses were Jewish. "Never heard of Jews then. They did speak with an accent like they were from somewhere else." Her mother always bought the shoes one size too big, so they could be worn longer, and there was no chance of the children getting new shoes before their old ones were completely worn out. "When I was a kid," said Wiseman, "what I really wanted in life was a cinnamon roll and a new pair of shoes from Bass's store. Everybody was happier then."

Each item also had a coded price tag, with a combination of letters that indicated the wholesale price next to the marked retail price. For Bass Mercantile, the code was "Best of Luck." The B equaled 1, the E equaled 2, the S equaled 3 and so on through K, which equaled zero. So a price tag with a BKK for the wholesale price meant the item cost $1.00. As a general rule, most items were marked up 50 percent, so an item that cost $1.00 at wholesale would probably go on sale at $1.50. The gross profit had to cover rent, utilities, shipping, clerical help, taxes and insurance. What remained was the store's net profit.

Over time, Nathan would give the children authority to bargain with customers over a price. Knowing the code, they could look at any price tag and be able to judge a price at which there would still be a decent profit. Typically, such bargaining would occur only if a customer was purchasing multiple items or a large volume.

At the end of his senior year in high school Jack looked for a summer job in Orangeburg to earn spending money for his coming year in college. But there was no seasonal work at a manufacturing plant, and the editor of the Orangeburg newspaper not only had no job to offer—he actively discouraged Jack from pursuing a career in journalism because the pay was generally so poor. With no job prospects in

---

66 Wiseman was interviewed by Ruth Bass Jacobs in Charleston.

Orangeburg, Jack turned to his father, who put him on the store payroll at $40 a week—a good salary in 1952.

Jack worked hard that summer. He cleaned toilets, swept floors, filled out monthly sales tax reports, made ledger entries and wrote checks to pay bills. He learned that Nathan's practice was to pay a bill early if it was "2/10, net 30," meaning he could take a two percent discount if he paid within 10 days. Jack worked at least 50 hours over a six-day work week, although he was allowed to leave early on baseball days to travel out of town with the North Pirates semipro team as their official scorer (he also pitched in a few games).

One of the problems of owning a business is finding time to take a vacation. With Jack working full-time at the store, Nathan showed great trust in his youngest son by taking a week off. Jack drove his parents to the Horowitz Kosher Inn in Hendersonville, North Carolina, dropping them off on a Sunday when the store was closed, then driving back to North to manage the store by himself. The following Sunday, Jack made the trip again, to bring his parents home.

That summer, Jack began eating dinner—the midday meal—at the North Hotel, which would serve roughly 25 people seated around two large tables. For 60 cents, plus two cents sales tax, Jack had his choice of two or three meats—fried chicken, beef stew, sliced ham or pork chops—and a selection of vegetables such as potatoes, rice and gravy, sliced tomatoes, potato salad, string beans, rutabaga, and squash. Biscuits, corn bread, dessert, and all the sweet iced tea one could drink (with ice chipped from a 50-pound block) rounded out the meal. Jack would eat everything they served except beets. "Everyone left with a full stomach and all of the town news and gossip of the day," Jack recalled. He would return to the store in good spirits, ready to work the rest of the day.

Bass Mercantile did well enough to support Nathan and Esther's large family with relative comfort by the standards of the time. While life in North was reasonably good for the Bass family, events in the rest of the world had turned in a direction that would eventually take its toll on them.

XII. The Nazi Stain Spreads Over Europe

As the 1930's came to a close, Nathan no doubt had mixed feelings about the state of the world. Despite the Depression, his family was doing well, relative to most. North was a quiet town, a good place to raise his children. The two older boys, Bernie and Herbie, were getting a college education, a privilege afforded to few in those days.

But Nathan knew that the world at large was not a happy place. As an avid reader of current events, including those reported in the Yiddish *Der Tag*, he was aware of the rapidly deteriorating situation in Europe and knew of the ongoing Japanese atrocities in China. Europe, in particular, would have worried him. Nathan still had many relatives living in Eastern Europe. It was no secret that the Nazis in Germany were persecuting Jews, taking away their rights and property and herding them into ghettoes as the anti-Semitic rhetoric from Hitler and his allies became ever more strident. Nazi sympathizers throughout Europe and Russia tried to imitate Hitler, making life uncomfortable for most Jews on the Continent.

While the official position of the English and French was to contain Hitler, there was little they could do militarily. Hitler tested them, invading Czechoslovakia with nothing more than loud diplomatic protestations from England and France. The United States, still slowly recovering from the Depression, did its best to stay out of European affairs. Jewish voters who'd supported Franklin Roosevelt lobbied for greater action against Germany. Congress was in no mood to get involved, but war planning and mobilization efforts proceeded.

Sitting in his easy chair at home, reading *Der Tag*, *Time*, *Reader's Digest*, *Life* and his daily newspapers, Nathan no doubt was worried. Little surviving correspondence with his relatives abroad exists. He no doubt got news from other relatives, in New York, or his brother Harry, in Lowell, with ties to the old country.

Of particular concern was his older brother, Noah Bass, the Jewish activist and Zionist living in Grodno. In 1935, the Jewish community of Grodno organized a "very festive party" in honor of Noah's 60th birthday "in which the greatest leaders of Zionism in Poland and the Land of Israel participated."[67] Shortly thereafter, Noah departed, for a second time, to Palestine, where his daughter Dina had settled. Noah planned to stay, but was not able to do so. At the time, Palestine was under British control. To stay in Palestine as a resident at the time, Jews were required to prove to the British governing authority that they had a means to support themselves, and Noah was not able to do so.[68]

Noah Bass and wife Elka.

---

67 See Noach Bass translation at 17.
68 See Noach Bass translation at 14, 17.

Noah's daughter Dina and her family in Israel.

Returning to Grodno, Noah continued his Zionist activities with the same passion as always. In 1936, however, the Polish government closed the Tarbut teachers seminary that Noah had helped found in Grodno in the 1920's.[69]

In 1939, as part of a deal between Hitler and Russian dictator Joseph Stalin, Poland was partitioned, with the Russians occupying the portion that included Grodno.

The Russian Communists immediately exercised political control.

> In Grodno all activity came to a halt. The [Jewish political] parties hid or burned their archives, and activists went into hiding. To ensure that they would not endanger the new regime by organizing resistance, the secret police arrested and, in some cases, exiled them. One of the victims of this policy was the Zionist activist

69 Lost Jewish Worlds; Between The World Wars-3, www.grodnoonline.org/lost_worlds/section_2c_test.html (accessed 12/18/10)

Noah Bass, who was arrested by the NKVD [Soviet secret police], interrogated, and ordered not to engage in Zionist activity.[70]

Noah was given a special restricted passport, for those the Russians deemed politically unreliable, that limited his travel at that point.

War was raging by now in Europe. Using "blitzkrieg" tactics, the Nazis invaded Belgium, Holland and France in quick order, while making alliances with Mussolini in Italy and Emperor Hirohito in Japan. The Germans took over much of central Europe. They began bombing England from the air. As the Nazis occupied country after country, they imposed their anti-Jewish restrictions and persecution, initial steps toward their horrific "final solution"—large concentration camps to serve as death factories for outright Jewish extermination. Top leaders in the United States were well aware of all this (although the developing full extent of activities in the concentration camps may not have been known early on), and yet, as 1941 progressed, still did little other than to offer "lend/lease" equipment to the beleaguered British, and then to the Russians after Hitler invaded their country.

Whether Nathan would have learned of it contemporaneously, we don't know, but in the summer of 1941, Noah and his wife Elka (a Yiddish school teacher) were again arrested by the Russians, along with large numbers of other Zionist Jews marked for deportation based on their special passports. The Germans had just started their invasion of Russian-occupied territory in Poland. Noah and the others were put on a train bound for Siberia. After traveling all night, the train was attacked early in the morning by German dive bombers, near the town of Baranowicz. The German planes came back and strafed the passengers fleeing the wreckage, killing many. Among the dead were Noah and Elka.[71] "My father wore white clothes in the summer time," said his son, Martin Bass, "and that made him a good target."[72] The date was June 24, 1941, and Noah was 67 years old.

---

70 Grodno Under Soviet Rule, 1939-41, www.eilatgordinlevitan.com/grodno/gr_pages/gr_stories_soviet.html (accessed 12/18/10)

71 See Felix Zandman, *Never The Last Journey*, Schocken Books, New York (1995) at p. 38. The account there was related by three survivors from the bombed train who made it back to Grodno on foot.

72 Interview of Martin Bass by Jack Bass, April 24, 1974, Atlanta, Georgia.

For the rest of the Bass family that had not emigrated, the German invasion was devastating. In 1939, border changes resulted in Vasilishok, located 90 miles northwest of Vilna, becoming part of Belarus, which had become a Nazi puppet state. The spelling of the name changed to Vasilishki. Formal German occupation began in June 1941 and Jews were soon thereafter forced to display yellow six-sided stars of David as Jewish identification badges, give up much of their property and move into a ghetto. Those who resisted would be shot summarily. Others would be killed for no reason at all, other than to terrorize the rest into submission.

———

Back in the United States, Nathan was well aware that Jews in Europe were being severely persecuted and executed. However, news from Eastern Europe after the German invasion would have been scant. It is doubtful that he learned of the fate of most of his and Esther's relatives, friends, and landsmen until much later in the war. He likely had not gotten word quickly on the death of his brother Noah. It was early in the German occupation and some Jewish refugees, carrying news with them, were still getting out. Among them was Michel Bass, Noah's youngest son, who got away on one of the last trains leading to England as borders closed behind him.

While Nazi forces were occupying Vasilishok and other parts of Eastern Europe in the summer of 1941, Bernie and Herbie Bass from North, South Carolina were volunteering for military active duty. Although the U.S. had not yet entered the war, it had been more than two years since Hitler made his initial military assaults in Europe in 1939, and to many Americans war appeared inevitable. The Jewish persecution at the hands of the Germans already was well begun when the Japanese attack on Pearl Harbor on December 7, 1941 finally caused the United States to enter the war. In the immortal words of President Franklin Roosevelt, it was "a day of infamy." The next day, Congress declared war on Japan. Japanese Admiral Yamamoto feared the attack on Pearl Harbor had "awoke[n] a slumbering giant." Two days later, Congress also declared war on Germany.

The United States was hardly ready for war. It would be nearly another year before U.S. troops would fight directly against the Nazis in any significant numbers, with the launching of Operation Torch in North Africa on November 8, 1942. In the Pacific, it was a different story, as the Japanese attacked a number of U.S. military bases and immediately invaded the Philippines. The U.S. had no choice but to fight the Japanese head-to-head following Pearl Harbor, whether ready or not.

Back at home, Americans rapidly mobilized for war. Tens of thousands of young men volunteered for service, and hundreds of thousands more followed in the draft. Some of them, like Bernie and Herbie, already had a head start, having joined earlier in anticipation of the inevitable showdown. Nathan no doubt understood that the world as he had known it was racing into a precipitous and dangerous transformation, and began to feel a quietly developing sense of deep loss.

XIII. The Bass Brothers Prepare For War

After graduating from North High School in 1934 as class valedictorian, Bernie attended the University of South Carolina in Columbia. Jack had been born just two months earlier, and Bernie was only sixteen years old. Bernie hitchhiked home each weekend to work in the store on Saturday—the day farm families typically came to town to do their shopping. A good student and hard worker, he wasn't immune to the problems that occasionally come up for a young man in college.

As a 16-year-old freshman, Bernie found himself in the middle of an investigation into an incident in which a drunken athlete tore down a door and damaged a dorm room. Called before the Dean of Men, Dr. Francis Bradley, Bernie refused to identify the athlete. It just so happened that Dean Bradley, a Southern gentleman of the old school, was also a professor of German. With Bernie facing discipline, Nathan drove to Columbia, entered Dean Bradley's office, greeted him in German (closely related to Yiddish) and discussed the entire situation, to Dean Bradley's delight, in German. A nominal reprimand closed the incident.[73]

After three years in college, Bernie enrolled in the law school, also at USC. After getting his law degree in 1940, Bernie set up a law office in North. But war was brewing and Bernie had already enlisted in the Army. Before his law practice could get established, Bernie received orders in June 1941 to report to an Army Air Corps training base in Cuero, Texas, where he would learn to fly.[74] The United States was not officially at war, but its involvement in the conflict was getting deeper by the day—America was supplying material to the English and other allies, and some veteran soldiers were already fighting in semi-autonomous units such as the Flying Tigers in China.

---

73 More than four decades later, Jack's three children all attended Francis Bradley Elementary School in Columbia, named for Dean Bradley.
74 See letter dated June 30, 1941 from Herbert Bass to Esther Robin.

Bernie's younger brother, Herbie, also headed off to the military at about the same time. As a teenager, Herbie exhibited a devilish, adventurous personality that contrasted with that of his older brother. Once, Herbie and a friend hopped a freight train to Savannah, Georgia where they planned to stowaway on a freighter to California. A friend of Nathan's in Savannah found the two sleeping on a park bench and talked them out of it. After spending all his high school graduation money, Herbie finally came home. On another occasion, Herbie and some friends barricaded the railroad tracks near North, forcing the "Silver Meteor" passenger train to stop. Once again, Nathan had to use his negotiating skills to talk the railroad's investigating agent out of having the boys arrested.

Herbie wanted to go to college, but times were tight. He begged his father to find the necessary funds. Referring to a boyhood pal who had been convicted of thievery, Herbie asked his father, "Do you want me to be like him?" Believing in education for his children, Nathan borrowed money from his brother Harry so that Herbie could enroll at The Citadel, South Carolina's military college in Charleston. Herbie responded well to the military discipline at The Citadel. He majored in business administration, attended ROTC camp in the summers, and obtained a private pilot's license. He also developed a love for classical music—on visits home he could be found listening to Brahms—or his favorite, George Gershwin's "Rhapsody in Blue"—in his spare time.

Herbie graduated from The Citadel with a B.A. in Business Administration at the end of the Spring semester in May, 1941, seven months before his 21st birthday.[75] With war in the air and Herbie filled with patriotism for his country, he enlisted in the Navy, officially joining on May 5, 1941.[76] Nathan had to sign for him to join since he wasn't yet 21. Herbie was soon off to the U.S. Naval Reserve Aviation Base in Atlanta, Georgia, for several weeks of basic training.[77] On November 13, 1941, he became an Aviation Cadet.

75 Lucille recalls that when Herbie graduated, she was at home with scarlet fever. Her mother told everyone, including her Aunt Fanny who was visiting for the graduation, that Lucille had the measles and wouldn't let anyone in to see her.
76 See Official Service Record of Herbert Bass.
77 Herbie tried to get Bernie to join the Naval Air Corps as well, but Bernie's army orders arrived before he could change his plans. See letter dated July 30, 1941 from Herbie Bass to Esther Robin.

Herbie and Bernie stroll down Peachtree Street in Atlanta.

For both Bernie and Herbie, the long training process was a new and exciting adventure. They wrote letters frequently, usually focusing more on their activities during "liberty"—leave from the base—than on anything else. For example, Bernie wrote to his father in July 1941 about a weekend trip to Victoria, Texas, where he saw a stage show and a movie, ate supper at the "best restaurant in town," then hung out with his buddies at "Club Reno" before finding a motel in which to spend the night.[78] Bernie's experience was no doubt similar to those of hundreds of thousands—and ultimately millions—of young men for whom the war was an opportunity to leave a small town and see other parts of the country,

78 Letter dated July 28, 1941 from Bernie Bass to Nathan Bass.

and then the world, that they may never have been exposed to in Depression-era America. They met their contemporaries from throughout the country, encountering new styles, customs, attitudes and cultures.

Herbie likewise enjoyed the opportunity to get off the base. In one letter to his cousin Esther Robin, a frequent correspondent, Herbie describes a weekend in Atlanta during which he saw a movie, went to the Cyclorama (depicting the Civil War Battle of Atlanta), stopped at the zoo, and had dinner at the Ship Ahoy restaurant, where his buddies had a lengthy "drinking party and bull session." Herbie claimed to have "stuck to Coca-cola" on account of his arm, which was sore from a typhoid shot he had received.[79] (Bernie, too, complained of soreness from his typhoid shot during his trip to Victoria, Texas.)

While Bernie and Herbie were off in training, their sister Lucille, then 11 years old, went off to South River, New Jersey to spend much of the summer with the Robin family and to spend some time in New York with her grandmother Rose Cohen and various of Esther's brothers and sisters there.

Herbie, too, took a break to visit with his northern relatives during that summer while waiting in Atlanta for assignment to actual flight training. First, Herbie stopped in Washington, D.C. to see his uncle Dave Cohn, then went on to New York to visit with his Aunt Fanny and Aunt Sadye. While in New York, he toured a factory that manufactured spark plugs for airplane motors. Herbie was surprised when the president of the company, for whom his mother had once worked, kept referring to her as "Emma Cohen," writing "I didn't know they ever called her that." Herbie ended up in South River, where Lucille already was visiting, before making a long trip back to Atlanta via a combination of hitchhiking and train rides.[80]

Although Herbie already had a pilot's license, Bernie was getting more flight time in the Army Air Corps early on. Describing one day when he did a few spins with his flight instructor, Bernie said it "beats any ride at the fair."[81] While Herbie languished in Atlanta, waiting for an assignment to flight training at Pensacola, Florida, Bernie was sent

---

79 Letter dated June 30, 1941 from Herbie Bass to Esther Robin.
80 See letter dated July 31, 1941 from Herbie Bass to Nathan and Esther Bass; letter dated August 9, 1941 from Herbie Bass to Esther Robin.
81 Letter dated July 28, 1941 from Bernie Bass to Nathan Bass.

to Maxwell Field, near Montgomery, Alabama for further flight training that would determine whether he would be a pilot. As fate would have it, however, Bernie washed out of flight school, which left him bitter and disappointed. He vented his frustration by writing about it in a piece prepared for submission to a magazine, but it was never published, which no doubt was just as well for his military career.

Bernie was hardly alone—becoming a pilot was an arduous process designed to winnow the few from the many. Each step of the way, a number of candidates would fail as the tests became more difficult. Bernie was still determined to fly, however, and so soon found himself bound for Mather Field in Sacramento, California, where he would get his training as a flight navigator.

Before reporting for further duty, Bernie had some time off, which he used to visit Herbie, now finally at the Naval Air Station in Pensacola, Florida. Whatever mixed emotions Bernie may have had that his younger brother would be a pilot, while he would not, were surely wiped out that day when they got together: it was December 7, 1941, the day of the Japanese attack on Pearl Harbor and the official start of the war for the U.S. Both young men were energized by the outbreak of hostilities, anxious to get into "action."

Just a few days after seeing Bernie, Herbie wrote home, stating quite presciently that "[t]his war is really going to be serious and deadly business for possibly the next four years." He also showed what he thought of anyone who didn't fully support the war effort: "any citizen who places him or herself above the country just isn't worth living." He added, "this war is truly a death struggle for everything that is worthwhile living for," and "easily worth everything we can possibly give."[82] The rambunctious teenager from North had grown into a serious young man within just a few short years of acquiring self-discipline at The Citadel.

Bernie, too, was ready to get going. Writing to his Aunt Sadye and Grandma Rose late in December, 1941, Bernie said "now that we are actually at war I am glad I started my training when I did. I only wish I had started earlier so I'd be commissioned now."[83] As it was, Bernie,

---

82 Letter dated December 13, 1941 from Herbie Bass to Nathan and Esther Bass.
83 Letter dated December 28, 1941 from Bernie Bass to Sadye Green and Rose Cohen.

who had just arrived at Mather Field, near Sacramento, California, had another 13-15 weeks of training to go, after which he would be commissioned a second lieutenant in the Army Air Corps as an aerial navigator "on the big bombers."[84]

As 1941 came to its dramatic close, Herbie managed to get four days of leave at Christmas time, making a 30-hour trek to North on the assumption that it would be his last trip home for some time. One of the things on Herbie's mind during that brief interlude was love. He dated a young woman there, well known to his family, wondering, in a subsequent letter to his cousin Esther, "whether there'd be much objection if I married a girl that wasn't Jewish." (He asked Esther to keep that between just the two of them.) "Mama's always lecturing to me that I should not even think of marrying anyone but a Jewish girl, but it seems to me that's exceedingly unreasonable. ... I think Mrs. Bass is going to be somewhat disappointed in her son one of these days."[85]

With the beginning of the new year, Herbie finally began flight training, noting his frustration that "it seems strange being in the Naval Air Corps for seven months and just starting to fly."[86] Aware of his brother Bernie's seemingly more rapid progress, Herbie lamented that "if I had joined the Army Air Corps last June, I'd have had my wings by this time and drawing about $150 per month more."[87]

Soon enough, the Bass boys would join the fight.

---

84 Id.
85 Letter dated December 30, 1941 from Herbie Bass to Esther Robin. Esther and Herbie continued to exchange correspondence on the issue of Herbie's dating the girl from North. In one of Herbie's letters a week later, he told Esther "there's not much correlation between love and reason," but that "there'll hardly be any danger of my getting married until this war's over" because "the Navy intends to keep us much too busy." Still, Herbie could "hardly imagine" the young lady "being married to anyone else." Letter dated January 6, 1942 from Herbie Bass to Esther Robin.
86 Letter dated December 30, 1941 from Herbie Bass to Esther Robin.
87 Letter dated January 6, 1942 from Herbie Bass to Esther Robin.

XIV. Holocaust In Europe

On May 9, 1942, according to official documents compiled at Yad Vashem, the Holocaust Memorial in Tel Aviv, the ghetto at Vasilishki (the name used for Vasilishok during the German occupation) was surrounded by Nazi troops. No one escaped. On May 10 and 11, people were taken in groups of 60 to the Jewish cemetery, where they dug mass graves and were ordered to undress and stack their clothes in piles. The naked men, women, and children were then pushed into the freshly dug ditches and shot--2,159 killed in those two days. A total of 2,865 of all nationalities died in Vasilishki, with another 598 sent off to Germany, where they presumably worked in slave jobs that few likely survived. German forces remained in Vasilishki until July 1944. All of Nathan's family members and landsmen who had remained in Vasilishki died at the hands of the Nazis. In 1967, an obelisk to "Soviet citizens" was erected to commemorate those killed by the Fascists; the memorial was later updated, in the 1990's, to indicate that the victims murdered there were Jews.[88]

Other relatives of both Nathan and Esther still living in the Pale generally suffered a similar fate. For example, German troops occupied Bialystok (where Esther was born), with its Jewish population of as many as 60,000, in June 1941. Three thousand Jews were burned alive the next month when they were locked in the Great Synagogue, the largest wooden synagogue in Eastern Europe, as it was set afire. By August, most Jews living in the Bialystok ghetto had been murdered or sent away.

Grodno, where Nathan had gone to cheder school with his brother Harry, shared a similar fate, being occupied in June 1941, shortly after Hitler declared war on the Soviet Union and invaded Russia. Although Nathan's older brother, Noah, was killed soon thereafter, he had two

---

88 See email dated March 21, 1998 to Ruth Jacobs re cemetery information from AJGS about Vasilishki.

sons, Mottl and Michel (Noah's sons by his second wife, Elka), who were still living in Grodno before the occupation. The younger of the two, Michel, managed to escape and get to London just before the Nazis invaded. The older, Mottl, had a much different fate.

Martin, Noah and Michel Bass.

Born in 1913, Mottl married Golda Skibelski and became a highly educated, successful lawyer, a young leader in Grodno's large Jewish community by the time the war broke out. What happened to Mottl—who later changed his name to Martin—and Golda is told in some detail in the book *Never the Last Journey*, by Felix Zandman, who survived the Holocaust and went on to become a successful American electronics entrepreneur.

After the Nazis took over Grodno in 1941, they forced all the Jews—30,000 at the time—into two small ghettoes. As was typical, the Germans made the Jews set up their own ghetto government, including Jewish police, a Jewish "mayor" and a group of "Farbindungsmen," Jews who worked as liaisons with the Gestapo. Mottl, with his legal background, became one of three Farbindungsmen in the Grodno ghettoes.[89] Working as a liaison with the Gestapo placed Mottl in a position of horrible conflict as he tried to do the best he could for his people.

At one point, the Germans announced their list of ghetto residents who would be transported to a nearby interim camp known as Kielbasin.[90] Felix Zandman's family was on the list, so his father went to Mottl to ask him to take them off the list. "Whom do you want me to put in your place?" asked Mottl. "We have to give them the number they have demanded." "Nobody," said Zandman's father in resignation, "put nobody in our place."[91]

While Mottl's position as a Farbindungsman protected him to some degree, he had no illusions that the Nazis would not, sooner or later, come after him as well. Throughout 1942 the Germans arranged "transports" in which significant numbers of Jews from the Grodno ghettoes were shipped away. Rumors of death camps abounded, but no one knew for sure.[92] What they did know was that no one ever heard anything again from those sent away. As the number of remaining Jews shrunk—most left behind were contributing some kind of special skills

---

89 *See* Never The Last Journey at 65.

90 Kielbasin started as a German camp for Soviet prisoners of war. It was later converted to a "transit" concentration camp, from which Jews were transported to Auschwitz and Treblinka. Many didn't survive that long: "The horrific conditions in the transit camps - overcrowding, inhuman living quarters, nonexistent sanitation, serious food shortages, bitter cold, and unspeakable filth - inevitably led to illness and epidemics. The mortality rate was high. Inmates were also subjected to all manners of harassments, beatings, abuse, and even outright murder by the staff and guards." *See* "Grodno Ghetto," http://deathcamps.org/occupation/grodno%20 ghetto.html, accessed October 21, 2009.

91 Never The Last Journey at 65.

92 One ruse the Germans used was to force deportees at Auschwitz to sign prepared postcards on which was printed, in German, "being treated well, we are working and everything is fine." The postcards were addressed to relatives in Grodno and sent out before the Jews in Auschwitz were murdered. See "Grodno Ghetto," http:// deathcamps.org/occupation/grodno%20ghetto.html (accessed Oct. 21, 2009).

to the German war effort—the Nazis closed the smaller ghetto and began contracting the larger one.

Jews in America were aware of the plight of their kin in Europe, although the full magnitude of the concentration camps was not known. Nathan's sister, Ida Bass Robin, gave a speech in Yiddish to a Hadassah chapter in her hometown of South River, New Jersey in 1942 while serving as chapter chairperson for the Jewish National Fund.

"In times like these," said Ida, "America, although at war, is the only country where we have the possibility to do the work and raise money to buy land in Palestine. And with God's help when the war will end and our brothers and sisters who will remain alive—I don't have to tell you that they are being shot on the battlefield, and that they are being hanged by the thousands only because they are Jews—should at least have a place to lay their heads down. We [are] the fortunate ones, who were lucky to come here in time and to raise our children in a free country, where they do not feel any difference of any kind that they are Jewish, and where they have the same rights as all other Americans. Our children do not know and cannot understand how much our sisters and brothers are suffering in Europe only because they were born Jewish."

Ida exhorted the women to teach their children that only by luck "were they born in a free country and the least they could do now is help with money to buy land in Israel." She urged that instead of sending flowers or telegrams for happy occasions or in memory of those who died, they should contribute to the Jewish National Fund and plant trees in honor of the living or in memory of the dead.[93]

One wonders whether Ida's involvement with the Jewish National Fund had anything to do with her older brother, Noah, who had stayed behind in Eastern Europe. The JNF was created in 1901 by the World Zionist Congress, a body in which Noah was active, to purchase land in what was then Ottoman Palestine, for Jewish settlement. Noah visited Palestine in 1905, and his daughter Dina settled there around 1920.

---

93 The speech was translated from Yiddish to English by Risa Bass, wife of Michel Bass, the son of Noah Bass who managed to escape to London before the Nazi occupation of Grodno, Michel stayed with relatives throughout the war, before emigrating to the U.S. afterwards. The portion of the speech quoted here is from an unpublished research paper, "Just Like One of Us," for independent study by Jack Bass, for Professor Allen Tullos at Emory University.

One of Noah's admirers in Grodno recalls that he "contributed, and he made others contribute, to the Jewish National Fund. . . . During the day he would go out for the benefit of the Jewish National Fund and it would be possible to see this man, with the grey hair and the blue box in his hand, call out to people to contribute to the Jewish National Fund."[94] One of the JNF's primary projects was the creation of forests in Palestine by planting millions of trees on arid soil that had limited agricultural potential, thereby improving the land for future generations of Jews. Over the years, the JNF project has resulted in tens of thousands of acres of forests in Israel through the planting of more than 200 million trees.[95]

Ida, like many Jewish immigrants from Eastern Europe, knew that a Jewish state in Palestine was probably the only hope for many of the Jewish survivors of the war then raging across the continent. She would soon be proud to see her nephews in America serving directly in that war against fascist aggression.

---

94 Noach Bass translation at 16.
95 See Wikipedia, "Jewish National Fund," (accessed 11/21/08): http://en.wikipedia. org/wiki/Jewish_National_Fund

XV. Bernie Fights The Nazis

By Spring 1942, Bernie had successfully completed his training. The newly minted 2d Lieutenant was assigned as a navigator/bombardier in a squadron of B-25 bombers that would soon be headed to North Africa, where American troops would have their first opportunity to battle the Nazi war machine head on.

Bernie Bass in uniform.

The B-25, named the "Mitchell" after General Billy Mitchell, an early advocate of air power and an independent Air Force, was a twin-engine medium range bomber used in every theater of WWII. A typical B-25 early in the war had a crew of six—a pilot, co-pilot, navigator who also served as bombardier, turret gunner who also served as flight engineer, a radio operator who also manned the waist gun, and a tail gunner. It would have been Bernie's job to navigate the plane to its target and then release its payload of bombs accurately on the enemy below. Americans flying these bombers in North Africa endured desert temperatures of as high as 118 degrees, sometimes with no shade but for the wings of their planes. In later missions over Europe, the slow moving B-25's took enormous amounts of punishment from enemy fighters and ground-based anti-aircraft fire. Joseph Heller's novel, *Catch-22,* and Stanley Kubrick's subsequent movie based on the book, were derived from the perilous missions of men flying B-25 bombers over Europe.

In North Africa the B-25 crews were somewhat more fortunate in that they were not flying over heavily fortified urban areas, nor were they dealing with large numbers of enemy fighter planes. Finding their targets, however, was more of a challenge, as they were sent to destroy enemy planes on the ground and to bomb Nazi armored formations— which would move about—instead of fixed targets such as railyards and factories. The Americans fighting in North Africa were privileged to become some of the first to strike back at the Germans, the vanguard of a much larger effort being mobilized at home.

By August, 1942, Bernie had made the long journey to Africa. In a letter to Herbie, he said, "I'm writing this sitting on my cot on the sand while native workmen are putting a cement floor on our tent." It was sufficiently dangerous that he wore "a 45 [caliber pistol] regularly, loaded with a couple spare clips on my cartridge belt." Subsisting on field rations, the men in Bernie's squadron were chipping in $10 apiece per month for better food—the natives were "learning how to cook to suit us a little better."[96] On August 27, 1942, Bernie went on his first bombing raid, a night action.[97] If Bernie was worried, he didn't show it—

---

96 Letter dated August 21, 1942, from Bernie Bass to Herbie Bass.
97 Letter dated August 27, 1942, from Bernie Bass to Herbie Bass.

instead he expressed frustration over delays in getting mail, a situation that made him "mad as hell."[98]

Soon, Bernie's squadron was busy, at one point in September making four daylight raids in the course of three days. But then things slowed down. Bernie received 48 hours leave for Rosh Hashanah, going to Cairo where he attended services conducted by a Jewish chaplain from the British Army. Before services were over, however, he got sick, ending up in a British hospital for five days with "sandfly fever," a malady that evidently afflicted just about everyone at some point.[99] Bernie's sisters, however, greatly appreciated the exotic leather hand-tooled pocketbooks he managed to purchase in Cairo and send back to them in North. Bernie also brought Lucille a scrapbook from Egypt, which she kept for years, finally giving it to Bernie's grandson Lee Michael on his bar mitzvah.

Being in North Africa not only gave Bernie a chance to bomb the Nazis, but also the opportunity to explore his Jewish heritage by going to Palestine. In October, Bernie sent his Grandmother Rose a postcard depicting the Great Synagogue in Tel Aviv after getting in a quick trip on a 48-hour leave.[100] Soon after, Bernie wrote home to say he'd be back in Palestine in a few weeks, when his crew would get a week-long leave, which would give him an opportunity to visit Jerusalem as well.[101] He also told his mother he'd lost about 15 pounds, putting him at a "perfect" weight of 151 pounds.

By this time, the United States had launched Operation Torch, a major land offensive in Northwest Africa aimed at Morocco, with the idea that it would clear the way for an invasion of Italy the following year. Bernie was probably flying missions in support of Operation Torch, as well as other Allied operations in the North African theater. At the time, American troops were working closely with the English, as well as

---

98 Id.

99 Letter dated September 17, 1942 from Bernie Bass to Lucille Bass. Sandfly fever is a flu-like condition caused by a viral infection transmitted by the bite of the female sandfly. See "Definition of Sandfly Fever," http://www.medterms.com/script/main/art.asp?articlekey=31320 (accessed Oct. 21, 2009).

100 Post card dated October 17, 1942 from Bernie Bass to Rose Cohn.

101 Letter dated November 17, 1942 from Bernie Bass to Esther Bass.

soldiers from all over the world. In Cairo, Bernie said he could count as many as 70 different uniforms while walking just one block.[102]

During one of his missions, in October 1942, Bernie's B-25 developed a problem while in flight. Bernie climbed down into the plane's cramped bomb bay to tighten a set of pins that had loosened on one of the bombs. For that act of valor, he received the Air Medal, which is awarded to any person who,"while serving in any capacity in or with the Armed Forces of the United States shall have distinguished himself/herself by meritorious achievement while participating in aerial flight."[103] As the year wound down, the North Africa campaign had achieved success, slowly grinding down some of Hitler's best troops, commanded by General Irwin Rommel, gradually pushing them out of the continent. The Allies were already looking ahead to an invasion of Italy, a first effort to put American troops on European soil.

---

102 "Davedevil Yank Fliers Yearn For, of All Things, Milk," copy of newspaper article, date missing.
103 See Wikipedia,"Air Medal," http://en.wikipedia.org/wiki/Air_Medal (accessed Oct. 21, 2009).

XVI. Herbie Itches For Real Action In The Pacific

While Bernie dropped bombs on Nazis, Herbie waited impatiently for his own chance to get into action. Not that what he was doing wasn't dangerous. During flight training at Pensacola early in 1942, Herbie explained to his cousin Esther Robin that flying "stunts" was actually pretty safe—"flying gets dangerous when one begins flying low and slow. Just about all the students and instructors who get killed here 'spin in' from a low altitude and therefore don't have any time to jump!"[104] Evidently, death held less fear for Herbie than the thought of some crippling injury. "A good thing about being in the Air Service is that you generally come back whole or not at all. In other words there's little chance of us being crippled after the war as there is in the land forces."[105]

---

104 Letter dated February 1, 1942 from Herbie Bass to Esther Robin.
105 Letter dated January 6, 1942 from Herbie Bass to Esther Robin.

To my dear Aunt and Uncle,
With love,
Herbert

Herbie Bass in uniform.

By March, 1942, Herbie had become a First Class Cadet. Photos of Herbie as a young military officer show him to be a dashing, handsome figure. With his devilish ways and outgoing personality, Herbie no doubt would have been popular with his peers. He was hoping—and expecting—to be assigned to duty in fighter planes. He was also waiting to see if he would get into the Marine Corps[106]. (Navy fliers typically flew off aircraft carriers, while the Marine fliers were usually based on land.)

At this point in time, the United States had its back against the wall with the Japanese in the Pacific theater of war. Following Pearl Harbor,

106 Letter dated March 2, 1942 from Herbie Bass to Esther Robin.

the Japanese invaded the Philippines, defeating American forces and taking tens of thousands captive. Other islands in the Pacific quickly fell, and the remnants of the U.S. fleet suffered a string of defeats. While Jimmy Doolittle's raid on Tokyo in April 1942 lifted American morale, it was militarily insignificant.[107] In May 1942 the Americans suffered an ignominious defeat in the Battle of the Coral Sea, where the aircraft carrier Lexington was sunk and the Yorktown severely damaged.

Not until the Battle of Midway, in early June 1942, did American forces achieve their first decisive victory in the Pacific. At Midway, U.S. carrier-based aircraft struck heavily at the Japanese fleet, sinking four aircraft carriers and wiping out a significant number of Japan's most experienced fliers. Perhaps the Battle of Midway made Herbie feel better about how he had fared: instead of fighter planes, he'd been assigned to a dive bomber squadron, and he made it into the Marine Corps as he had hoped—on May 29, 1942 in Miami, Florida, he executed the oath of office as a Second Lieutenant in the Marine Corps Reserve (effective **[to]** May 1, 1942).

At Midway, dive bombers played a pivotal role. An initial attack by Marine dive bombers based on the island fared poorly, the Marines losing most of their planes in an ineffective attack. The battle turned, however, when a flight of carrier-based Navy Douglas SBD Dauntless dive bombers—also called the "Banshee" in the Army's version—caught the Japanese off guard and scored several direct hits on at least three of the Japanese carriers.

When the Battle of Midway was fought, Herbie was still in the United States, continuing his training while awaiting assignment to a combat unit. He was at Camp Kearney, near San Francisco, where he'd been assigned to Marine Scout Bombing Squadron 142 (VMSB 142). In August, Herbie got himself in a bit of trouble, earning five days of arrest (confined to quarters) "for disobedience of orders relative to proper functioning of radio equipment prior to

---

107 Doolittle's crews trained in Columbia, South Carolina and flew a modified version of the B-25 Mitchell bomber, the same plane in which Bernie Bass was flying in North Africa. While home on leave, Bernie took young Jackie with him to Columbia to visit the base where Doolittle's crews were training. That base was on the site of today's Columbia Metropolitan Airport.

take off."[108] That incident didn't seem to hold him up for long, however. A few days later, on August 22, Herbie was sailing with his unit aboard the M.S. Bay Star from San Diego to Pearl Harbor.[109] From there he was transferred to Midway Island—"1000 miles from the nearest civilization."[110]

Herbie had reached the Pacific, but the fighting had moved further south, to the Solomon Islands, particularly a miserable little jungle isle known as Guadalcanal. Life on Midway was relatively cushy, especially compared to that of Herbie's fellow Marine fliers who were just then arriving at Henderson Field on Guadalcanal. Herbie lived with five other men in a dugout covered with sand, which had electricity, but no running water.[111] On Guadalcanal, pilots lived in tents with no floors, no electricity and no water.[112]

Midway had a fully functioning air field. In contrast, Henderson Field, which had been taken from the Japanese by Marine troops while it was still under construction, was a rudimentary facility. The squadron operations office at Henderson Field was a "dugout with sandbags and coconut logs and then covered with dirt."[113] The "control tower" at the field consisted of four palm logs supporting a small platform about 50 feet in the air, from which a pilot would operate a telephone and shoot off red and green roman candles as signals to incoming planes as to whether it was safe to land. Life on Guadalcanal was extremely dangerous during that initial period: when the first squadron of dive bomber pilots was relieved at Guadalcanal on October 12, 1942—less than two months after arriving—only one of its twelve pilots was still able to fly, the rest having been killed or wounded.

Meanwhile, for Herbie, Midway was almost a vacation. "There are no uniform requirements; each man wears what he damn well pleases, anywhere from bathing trunks on up." A lot of the men grew beards

---

108 Official Marine Service Record of Herbert Bass (sheet 1).
109 Id.
110 Letter dated September 23, 1942 from Herbie Bass to his parents.
111 The descriptions of Herbie's life on Midway come from a letter he sent home, dated September 23, 1942.
112 Descriptions of life for pilots on Guadalcanal come from McEniry, "A Marine Dive Bomber Pilot at Guadalcanal," University of Alabama Press, 1989.
113 Marine Dive-Bomber Pilot at 25.

and/or mustaches. They had "a lot of free time in which [they could] read, play cards, ball, ping-pong, checkers, etc.," They also had "a first rate beach 200 yards away" where Herbie would go almost every day, "no bathing suits necessary." Herbie thought the "chow" was "o.k." On the downside, there were "no women, no liberty, no nothing within you know how far [1000 miles]". With time on his hands, Herbie wrote to his mother, asking her to send him his favorite "Rhapsody in Blue" records.

While Herbie restlessly waited on Midway, the bitter fighting in and around Guadalcanal raged for several months. Throughout the period, Japanese ships of all kinds sought to re-supply and reinforce their troops on the island, and it was the job of the Marine Dauntless pilots to try to sink those ships when they were spotted.

In November, 1942, Marine dive bombers played a decisive role in preventing the Japanese from launching a major offensive to retake Guadalcanal. On the night of November 12-13, the U.S. Navy suffered severe losses in a major sea battle with Japanese forces, losing a number of cruisers and destroyers in a night battle that lit up Henderson Field for hours. As a result of the battle, the Navy was in no position to stop the Japanese from landing 11 troop transports with 12,500 crack soldiers on the Island.

The next night, General Louis E. Woods, the new Marine Air Commander for Guadalcanal, told the Marine dive bomber pilots that they were all that was standing between the Island and the fresh Japanese troops. Failure to stop them would likely mean evacuation of the U.S. forces stationed there. "We lay the fate of Guadalcanal in your hands and know that each of you will do his best," said the General, in closing.[114]

Shortly thereafter, the field was shelled for more than an hour by two heavy Japanese cruisers, destroying a number of planes and rattling the pilots and crews. As tension mounted, word filtered back to Washington, where it was already morning, that Japanese transports were heading down the "slot"—the sea lane between various Solomon Islands leading to Guadalcanal—without opposition from surface ships. "The tension that I felt at that time," recalled Navy Secretary Forrestal, "was matched only by the tension that pervaded Washington the night before the landing in Normandy."[115]

---

114 Marine Dive Bomber Pilot at 60.
115 Id. At 63.

As dawn broke on November 14, Marine pilots began their searches for enemy shipping, soon sending in reports of sightings of many vessels, including an aircraft carrier, a battleship and numerous cruisers and destroyers. At 6:30 a.m., the first wave of Marine dive bombers took off to attack the main Japanese task force, with the troop transports now less than 150 miles away. Wave after wave of Dauntless dive bombers from two Marine squadrons and a Navy squadron that had come over from the crippled aircraft carrier Enterprise, braved anti-aircraft fire and Japanese fighters to press the attack. When they were done, six transports were sunk, one was damaged so badly it had to turn back, and only four were left.

The next morning, delayed by yet another nighttime naval battle, the four transports were beached to unload their cargo of troops and equipment. Marine dive bombers struck again, setting at least two ships on fire and killing many Japanese soldiers. Later reports indicated that only 2,000 Japanese troops made it ashore, not enough to turn the tide against the growing American force on the Island. Afterward, President Roosevelt remarked, "It would seem that the turning point in the war has been reached."[116] Never again would the Japanese engage in an offensive operation in WWII.

No doubt, Herbie was proud of his fellow Marine dive bomber pilots, some of whom he likely had trained with at some point. While the Marine pilots on Guadalcanal were fighting a battle of life and death, however, Herbie and his fellow pilots waiting on Midway were having their pictures taken. A Life Magazine photographer spent several days on the island in September, with his article appearing in the November 23, 1942 edition. Herbie wasn't pictured, but some of his fellow pilots were. "I was among the more than half unlucky ones whose mug was not included," Herbie wrote with obvious disappointment to his cousin Esther. "Of us ten pilots who came out in September, only three got their pictures in."[117] But his plane made it in: "I was flying plane no. 5 in that picture above the reef."[118]

---

116 Id. At 75.
117 Letter dated December 2, 1942 from Herbie Bass to Esther Robin. Both Herbie and Bernie were avid bridge players, card games being a frequent activity in the Bass household. Herbie described one evening on Midway when he and his mates spent six straight hours playing bridge, "which was overdoing it."
118 Letter dated December 12, 1942 from Herbie Bass to Esther Robin.

Indeed, *Life* devoted seven full pages of photos to the Marines of Midway. The opening photo, taking up an entire page, was the one to which Herbie referred, showing at least part of nine Dauntless dive bombers flying over Midway's coral reef.[119] The last page of the photo spread included pictures of twelve Marine fliers, including three who Herbie knew well: John Stock, Julius Bercik and Henry White.[120] *Life's* photographer, however, had taken a nice picture of Herbie, adjusting his headgear while standing beside the cockpit of a dive bomber. The magazine later provided a copy of the photo to the Bass family.

Herbie's squadron flying over Midway Island.

It was also Gooney Bird season on Midway. Herbie described the large members of the albatross family as a "beautiful bird with a wing-spread of about six feet ... they are the most fearless and comical of all birds." Herbie anticipated that by the end of November there would be

119 Life Magazine, Nov. 23, 1942, p. 118.
120 Id. at p. 130. In June 1943, Stock and several other pilots were forced to ditch their planes in a lake on one of the other Solomon Islands after a raid on a Japanese airfield. They were eventually rescued after the native chief gave them shelter in his village. Marine Dive-Bomber at 136-157.

upwards of a hundred thousand of the birds on the island, a federally protected sanctuary.[121]

Herbie could feel his time for action coming. He got his own plane late in November, contemplating naming it "North Star." In a letter to his Uncle Victor and Aunt Ida, Herbie lamented that Bernie, who he'd recently heard from, was "in the thick of things" and wished that "I could see some real action for a change."[122] Many of the other pilots he'd been with at Midway—including some of those in the Life Magazine story—were already at Guadalcanal, and Herbie expected "to be joining them shortly."[123]

Before going off to the Solomon Islands, however, Herbie got one last opportunity for leave around Christmas. He went to Hilo, on the Big Island of Hawaii, staying at a hotel "right below snow-capped Mauna Kea." He told his cousin Esther Robin that it was the "most beautiful spot" he'd ever been to.[124]

At home in North, Nathan and Esther must have been proud of their two boys—and at least a little relieved—as 1942 came to a close. There was much fighting yet to be done, but Bernie and Herbie were out there, doing their patriotic duty for the United States of America with distinction.

---

121 Letter dated November 29, 1942 from Herbie Bass to Esther Robin.
122 Letter dated November 29, 1942 from Herbie Bass to Victor and Esther Robin.
123 Letter dated December 12, 1942 from Herbie Bass to Esther Robin.
124 Post card dated December 22, 1942 from Herbie Bass to Esther Robin.

XVII. The War At Home

On Sunday afternoons, North's white youths would park their cars on Main Street by the railroad track and hang out with each other, or drive by slowly to see who was hanging out with whom. That's where Frances was on Sunday, December 7, 1941 when she heard about Pearl Harbor being bombed. The next day the entire school assembled in the auditorium to listen to President Roosevelt's speech declaring war. Frances's English teacher, Mrs. Nussbaum, wept openly because her fiancé was in the Army.

While Bernie and Herbie were off at war, life went on in North. Gasoline and many food items were rationed, but Nathan still managed to take his family back and forth to Columbia most weekends for Sunday school at the Tree of Life Temple. He regularly picked up hitchhikers along the way, and if they were soldiers and the family was headed home, Nathan invariably invited them to dinner.

Every day the children raced over to the Post Office, hoping to get mail from either Bernie or Herbie. They also frequently wrote letters to their brothers away at war.

Business at the store was good, with the girls all helping out. Bernie urged his mother not to work too hard, but then recognized "that you and daddy thrive on work when there is something doing. In a store, as in the Army, it is sitting around that gets you down."[125]

North had its own role in the war, too. As the battle progressed, the Army Air Force built a landing field near North with a 10,600 foot long, 500 foot wide runway, designed to handle projected new and larger bombers coming into production. A couple of the construction workers on the project lived in the little apartment behind the Bass house—the room that had been Bernie's before the War.[126] Lucille recalls cleaning

---

125 Letter dated Nov. 17, 1942 from Bernie Bass to Esther Bass.
126 One of the workers, Charlie Millard, took a fancy to Frances, but they did not date at that time (Nathan would not let his daughters date anyone who wasn't Jewish). Later, while Frances was at the University of South Carolina, Charlie was in the Naval ROTC there and they dated a bit, including going to the formal ROTC

out the room to make it available to the new men, and finding stacks of Life Magazines stored there.

It was a busy time for the older girls—both Ruth and Frances enrolled in college at "Carolina"—the University of South Carolina in Columbia. Attending with Ruth was her cousin Miriam Robin, from New Jersey, who had turned down an offer from Duke to attend Carolina and be with her cousins.

Miriam Robin Greyson and husband Jonah.

---

ball together. After the war, Charlie went back to a job he'd held at Cates Pickles and sent a case of pickles to the Bass family, but Nathan refused the delivery because he was afraid Charlie wanted to court Frances.

The other worker, Raymond Bost, who was the son of the owner of the construction company building the base, later became a minister, and then president of Lenoir Rhyne College in Hickory, North Carolina. When Frances's youngest daughter, Sally, attended Lenoir Rhyne many years later, Raymond was delighted to see Frances again.

The younger children had some changes in their schedules due to the War. School started later in the year so that students could help pick cotton—for half a cent a pound—since many of the local men were off in the military. Lucille recalls volunteering to help once and going into the fields with a white bag—her only time cotton picking. Cotton picking is hard work and it probably didn't sit too well with a "town" girl like Lucille, whose earnings amounted to less than a dime.

Lucille looked forward to Bernie's visits home, when he would bring gifts from his exotic travels. Or he would use his money, saved up in the military to buys things for his sisters, such as going to the nearby town of Barnwell and purchasing dresses for them at the Levinsons' store there.

Nylon was one of many rationed items, which meant that nylon stockings were hard to get. The Bass children ingratiated themselves with their teachers during the war by giving out nylon stockings as Christmas presents since Nathan had access to some from his store.

Overall, life wasn't that much different in North, especially compared to other parts of the world. But for Nathan and Esther, with two sons in the war, and many relatives likely dying in Europe, times were stressful.

XVIII. A Sliver Of Hope In Europe

By early 1943 the number of Jews remaining in Grodno was down to fewer than 8,000 (out of approximately 21,000 before the war), all crammed into a tiny ghetto. On Friday, February 13, 1943, the Nazis sealed the ghetto as they started selecting another group of Jews for "transport." One of those selected was Sender Freydovicz, who was Felix Zandman's uncle. Instead of meekly standing in the line for certain death, Sender bolted down a narrow street, dodging gunfire and hiding in a narrow alley. A Jewish policeman found him there and suggested a better hiding place. Soon, Sender secreted himself in a toilet room in the apartment building where Mottl Bass lived.[127]

Later in the day, Mottl opened the door, startled to find Sender there, clutching a brick with which to club his pursuers. "You know they're searching for you all over," said Mottl. "There's an order for you to be hung. You've got to get away from here." Sender told Mottl he had a place in mind, but first he needed Mottl to retrieve a five-ruble gold piece from Sender's brother Kushka (who had been exempt from the transport). What happened next is told by Zandman:

> When Bass came back with the money, Sender told him, "Look, you know better than anybody what's going on. You know they're eventually going to kill you, too, just like they're killing everybody else. I've got this place I'm going to, at least until the transport is over. I think maybe they'll hide you and your wife, too, for a day or so. If you want, you can come there." Then he told him about Janova Puchalski's.

---

127 Unless otherwise noted, the information in this chapter is from Zandman, *Never The Last Journey* (Schocken Books, 1995).

That night, Sender escaped, making his way to the home of a Polish peasant family, Jan and Janova Puchalski, in the tiny village of Lossossna,[128] not far from Grodno. The Puchalskis had been caretakers of vacation dachas owned by the family of Zandman's mother, and the two families had shared strong bonds over the years despite their ethnic and religious differences. Once, when Janova was pregnant, her husband had thrown her out in a drunken rage. Turning to her Jewish landlord, Janova was taken in, given a place to live and eventually allowed to give birth to her child in the Jewish hospital in Grodno, for which she had been ever grateful.

When Sender arrived at the Puchalski's home, his nephew, Felix was already there, having had the same thought and arrived a day earlier. The two spent a day in the Puchalski's attic, trying to figure out what to do next. The following night, Janova poked her head into the attic and said, "Come down. Four of your friends just arrived."

> When we got downstairs there were Mottl Bass; his wife Goldie; Borka Shulkes, another Farbindungsman; and Meir Zamoszczanski, one of the Jewish policemen. That made thirteen people in the house, the seven Puchalskis and now all of a sudden six of us. "It's too many," said Janova. "You have to go outside, to the potato cellar."
>
> The potato cellar, out back about thirty yards from the house, was pitch dark and full of potatoes that felt like stones as we all tried to find some comfortable way of sitting or lying down. When we did, Bass told Sender and me what had happened.
>
> After Sender left, Bass had talked the situation over with his wife. They knew Sender was right. Their turn was coming, Farbindungsman or no Farbindungsman. This transport was clearing out most of those who had survived the "transport of ten thousand" a month earlier. After this, Bass thought, only a couple of thousand would be left, and how long would the Germans let them live?

---

128 The Lossossna train depot was used to transport Jews from the transit camp at Kielbasin to Auschwitz and Treblinka. See "Grodno Ghetto," http://deathcamps.org/occupation/grodno%20ghetto.html (accessed Oct. 21, 2009).

Bass knew where the Freydovicz summer houses were, and he trusted Sender's word about being allowed to stay at the Puchalskis[']. But with all the Germans around and a transport going in he didn't know if he and his wife could get out by themselves. They would have a better chance with the help of a Jewish policeman. So Bass went to Meir Zamoszczanski and told him that they had a place to hide outside the city. If Zamoszczanski could get them out, he could come with them. He also told Borka Shulkes, the second Farbindungsman, who was a good friend of his. Shulkes said that his wife was already in hiding outside the city; he was looking for a way to escape the ghetto and join her. Maybe Zamoszczanski could get the three of them out.

That was how the Basses, Shulkes, and Zamoszczanski had ended up at the Puchalskis'. Now we had to decide what to do. The potato cellar had no future as a hiding place. Food would have to be brought in and out, assuming we could find a way of getting food. The Puchalskis could barely keep their own children fed. There would have to be a way to get excrement out. With six people living there, somebody would be sure to notice suspicious activity. Besides, the place was obvious. If anyone suspected Jews might be hiding with the Puchalskis, the potato cellar would be the first place they'd look.

What the refugees didn't know was that their escape had caused recriminations back in Grodno. Upon learning that the two farbingdungsmen had slipped out of the ghetto, the Nazi commander of the ghetto, Kurt Wiese, ordered the remainder of the Judenrat—the Jewish governing council—rounded up. He then shot their leader, David Brawer (who had been headmaster of the local Jewish tarbut school that he had co-founded with Noah Bass) in front of the synagogue.[129]

---

129 Grodno Ghetto, http://deathcamps.org/occupation/grodno%20ghetto.html (accessed Oct. 21, 2009). Mottl later told Felix that the Zionist Tarbut teachers in Grodno had formed a rudimentary resistance organization in the ghetto, which had managed to smuggle a few people to the partisans in the forests. But the resistance

For the refugees in the potato cellar, the solution to their immediate problem was to dig a cellar inside the Puchalski home. After two nights of work, careful to conceal the activity from neighbors, the refugees had managed to make a hole about five feet wide, five and a half feet long and four feet deep in which to hide. Imagine six people trying to live in such a hole, which Felix Zandman—then a teenager—said "looked like a grave." After a couple of days, it became clear that the space was too small for six. Following some discussion, Shulkes and Zamoszczanski agreed to leave—they had viewed this as a temporary stop in any event. Sender talked to Janova, who agreed that Mottl and Goldie could stay.

Fortunately, Mottl had money with him—a number of twenty-dollar gold pieces he was carrying in a money belt. The gold pieces had previously been sown into the hem of one of Goldie's dresses to hide them. Mottl and Sender agreed that it should be given to Janova one piece at a time so she would have enough money to purchase food for the extra mouths to feed. But Sender only agreed after a tense moment in which he confronted Mottl about where he'd gotten the money. Mottl assured him it was from a relative, not from bribes Sender suspected he might have taken as a Farbindungsman. Since all the gold pieces were identical, Sender accepted Mottl's story, deducing that bribe money would be in all different forms.

It was February, 1943. Although the refugees were aware that Germany had suffered a major defeat in Stalingrad just a few weeks earlier, there still was no sign that the Soviets, or the Allies, would—or even could—push the Germans back anytime soon. Mottl and Goldie Bass settled in for what they anticipated would be a long wait. Their hosts, the Puchalskis, were at equal peril—if caught hiding Jews, their entire family would be killed by the ruthless Nazis.

---

group had gotten no support from the rabbis or Brawer. Instead, these natural community leaders had counseled patience, keeping everyone's heads down, in the hope that, like the pogroms of old, this would pass and most would survive. *Never The Last Journey* at 108.

XIX. Tragedy In The Pacific

While the Jews remaining in Europe were hiding or fleeing for their lives, Herbie Bass was finally getting his wish to see some action in the Pacific. On New Year's Day, 1943, Herbie wrote home:

Dear Folks,

Have traveled quite some distance since last writing you. Am now well below the equator and past the international date line. About 9000 miles from the East Coast. The days are very long and hot down here as this is the summer season. We have a lot of trouble with mosquitoes, but it's not too bad.[130]

Herbie was on Guadalcanal, at long last. He had just turned 22 on what was the "shortest birthday anniversary of my life"—because he crossed the international dateline on December 27, his birthday, it had been only 12 hours long. Soon after he arrived on Guadalcanal, Herbie received a promotion to 1st Lieutenant.[131] The good news was that the intensity of fighting in and around Guadalcanal was tapering off. Reading about it in his various newspapers and magazines must have eased some of Nathan's fears.

Piloting a Dauntless dive bomber in combat, however, was a dangerous task requiring tremendous skill and courage. Pilots and crews swore that "SBD" stood for "slow but deadly." When fully loaded with

---

130 Letter dated January 1, 1943 from Herbie Bass to Nathan and Esther Bass. Neither Herbie nor Bernie would have been allowed, by military censors, to say exactly where they were stationed in any of their correspondence home. From Herbie's descriptions, it is likely that Nathan would easily have guessed where his second son was.

131 See letter dated February 1, 1943 from Esther Robin to Herbie Bass, which was later returned undelivered, congratulating him on his promotion.

up to two thousand pounds of bombs, the Dauntless was indeed slow, making for easy pickings by the dreaded Japanese Zero fighters. To ward off enemy fighters, the SBD's would try to fly in a formation of at least six planes, arranged so that their rear seat gunners could cover all angles of potential attack.[132]

Japanese naval anti-aircraft fire was also often effective against the Dauntless once it began its dive because the plane could not take evasive action at that point. When making a bombing run, a Dauntless pilot would descend at terminal speed—240 knots (275 mph)—from an altitude of as high as 12,000 feet. From there it would take 25-30 seconds to reach the release point, at about 1,500 feet. At that point, the pilot would pull the bomb release and immediately begin a sharp pullout while closing the dive brakes that stabilized the plane during its rapid descent. Invariably, the "G forces" of pulling out of the dive were so great that the pilots would go into some stage of a blackout—temporarily losing sight. All this while being shot at by enemy anti-aircraft batteries.[133]

Herbie would soon be facing the test of his life in this deadly environment.

Meanwhile, Bernie was still in Africa. In a letter home dated February 12, 1943, Bernie stated that he'd seen "surprisingly little action" over the past two months. That week, General E. W. (Big Ed) Timberlake arrived at the field where Bernie was stationed and presented him with the Air Medal he had earned for his courageous service back in October, 1942. Bernie told his parents that he had seen General Hap Arnold— "the chief of the entire Army Air Force"—a month earlier when he visited Bernie's field base. Arnold "talked with our squadron for about an hour. He is a wonderful man. He let us do practically all the talking, just asked questions about things."

Bernie was anticipating another trip to Palestine with his upcoming leave, during which he intended to look up his cousin Dina Gan, Noah Bass's oldest daughter, from his first marriage. Dina had settled in Palestine with her husband in 1920 and so would have been an excel-

---

132 Much of the information in this section is from McEniry, "*A Marine Dive-Bomber Pilot At Guadalcanal*" Univ. Alabama Press (1987).
133 Id. At 21-22.

lent guide to the holy land for Bernie.[134] It is not likely that Dina knew the plight of her half-brother Mottl back in the woods near Grodno, although she certainly would have believed he was in grave danger if he was, indeed, still alive.

In January, 1943, Herbie's unit, VMSB-142, was quite active around Guadalcanal, providing "support bombing in preparation for the Army advance" on Japanese positions.[135] On January 15, the squadron made a bombing attack on nine Japanese destroyers. Five days later, two planes in the squadron collided in mid-air, killing the gunner in one, but remarkably ending in no other injuries.[136]

The squadron's combat tour was winding down. By month's end, all pilots and gunners from VMSB-142 would be evacuated to Espiritu Santo and then to Sydney, Australia for rest and recreation. Before that, however, Lt. Herbert Bass was sent on a mission, on January 22, 1943, in search of the infamous "Pistol Pete," the nickname given to the Japanese artillery battery that periodically shelled Henderson Field and various army positions on Guadalcanal. He didn't have his usual gunner with him that day. Instead, he had Corporal Alfred Francis Hozempa, of Pennsylvania, who was with VMSB-273.[137]

Whether Herbie and Alfred found Pistol Pete will never be known. They didn't return from their mission that day. The following day, another plane was sent out to look for them, and found the badly smashed wreckage of their plane in a river behind Japanese lines. It appeared that Herbie's plane had been hit by enemy fire, after which he tried to land in the river. There was no sign of Herbie or Alfred, and "the possibility of survival looked very slim."[138]

---

134 Letter dated February 12, 1943 from Bernie Bass to Esther Bass.

135 The History of Marine Scout Bombing Squadron 142, www.dauntlessdivebombers.com/VMSB-142History.html (accessed 12/18/10).

136 Id.

137 See Certificate of Death for Alfred F. Hozempa. The certificate also contains an interesting note that the plane flown by Herbie that day was "supposedly attached to [the] USS Enterprise." A dive bomber on the aircraft carrier Enterprise would be a Navy plane, but it was not unusual for planes to be mixed up when, for example, an aircraft carrier was damaged.

138 See letter dated June 14, 1944 from Alphonse Hozempa to Mrs. Nathan Bass.

On a Sunday morning,[139] an ominous telegram arrived at the Bass household. Telegrams seldom brought good news, and this was no exception. The telegram stated that Lt. Herbert Bass was missing in action. He and the gunner in his plane had failed to return from an attack mission from Guadalcanal. The Bass household was shattered. It was the worst possible news, leaving the family in limbo, wanting for more information, fearing the worst, yet holding out hope that their handsome, gregarious son was somehow still alive.

When the news came in, Ruth was a sophomore at Carolina and Frances a freshman. Ruth called Frances, who was in the freshman dorm, to come over to her dorm—Sims House. Their cousin Miriam Robin, also a sophomore, was already there. The three sat on the floor and talked to Mama Bass in North. No doubt they cried. Later that day they were on a train home, in a state of shock.

Word spread quickly through the small community of North. A steady stream of visitors, mostly friends and neighbors, came by the house, many bearing dishes or baskets of food. Jack, the youngest—then age eight—recalls being sent out to play with friends, numb with shock but not yet able to comprehend the depth of loss. It's not clear how long it took for word to get to Bernie, but the news undoubtedly distressed Herbie's older brother out in the desert of North Africa.

Letters of condolence and sympathy came pouring in, many from the Jewish community of merchants around South Carolina. A "Uniongram" arrived from Helen Kohn Hennig in Columbia; Hyman Rubin, of J. Rubin & Son Co. in Columbia, sent a note after learning the news from Mr. Schechter; Shep Pearlstine, wholesale grocer in St. Matthews, sent a letter after reading in the newspaper that Herbie was missing in action; Sally and Abe Cohen wrote from Ninety Six, S.C., where they had a department store.[140] Other letters came from non-Jews who knew the Bass family and had done business with Nathan, such as R.A. Goolsby, "Express, Truck & Carlot

---

139 We don't have the date of the telegram, but judging by condolence letters sent to the Bass household in early March 1943, it was probably Sunday, February 28, 1943.

140 See letter dated March 3, 1943 from Helen Kohn Hennig to Mr. & Mrs. Nathan Bass; letter dated March 2, 1943 from Hyman Rubin to Mr. & Mrs. Bass; letter dated March 8, 1943 from Shep Pearlstine to Mr. & Mrs. N. Bass; letter dated March 3, 1943 from Sally & Abe Cohen to Mr. & Mrs. Bass.

Dealer" in Denmark, S.C.[141] The President of The Citadel also wrote with a sentiment, shared in much of the correspondence, to keep up the family's hope: "While, of course, I should not want to raise any false hopes I know from my own battle experience that many, originally reported missing in action, actually later turn up safe and sound."[142]

For Esther, the news was devastating. She became withdrawn. She would go through the house and throw out things of his. Lucille, still being at home, noticed the changes and felt that her mother suffered from not having any really close friends in North. Jack, the youngest, also felt the withdrawal, not only by Esther, but even more from Nathan, who he felt gave him little attention after Herbie was declared missing, together with his developing awareness of the horror of the Holocaust wracking Europe.

Almost a year later Nathan received a letter from Marine Captain Josephus Daniels, Jr.[143] that a full review of "the circumstances surrounding [Herbie's] disappearance indicates a possibility that he may be alive and a prisoner of war and that his status would remain as missing in action."[144] In response to a letter from Nathan, Captain Daniels wrote another letter, in March 1944, stating that a portion of Herbie's allotment would be continued because "the obvious purpose of the major portion of it is for the support of his sister"—Frances—while attending college at Carolina. Daniels asked Nathan to furnish a summary of Frances' estimated monthly expenses.

Although Daniels' letter gave the family some hope that Herbie was alive—along with the dread that he could be a Japanese prisoner-of-war—

---

141 See letter dated March 7, 1943 from R.A. Goolsby to Mr. & Mrs. N. Bass.

142 See letter dated March 5, 1943 from C.P. Summerall to Mr. Nathan Bass.

143 Captain Daniels was the son of a former Navy Secretary in the Woodrow Wilson administration, from 1914-21, and former Ambassador to Mexico in the Franklin Roosevelt administration. The senior Josephus Daniels had risen to prominence as the editor of the Raleigh News and Observer, and although he served in progressive Democratic administrations, he had advocated white supremacy and black disenfranchisement in his newspapers around the turn of the century. Under Josephus, Jr., however, the newspaper became a voice of moderation in the civil rights era. See Wikipedia, "Josephus Daniels," http://en.wikipedia.org/wiki/Josephus_Daniels (accessed October 14, 2009).

144 The information in this and the following paragraphs is taken from an unpublished research paper, "Just Like One of Us," written by Jack Bass for an independent study course with Professor Allen Tullos at Emory University.

the family soon received additional information that indicated Herbie's survival unlikely. After learning the name of the enlisted gunner who flew with Herbie on his last flight, Esther Bass wrote to his family in Pennsylvania. The gunner's brother, Alphonse Hozempa, responded, reporting a first hand account from a friend of his brother, which confirmed that Herbie "was the pilot of the plane that went out on that fateful morning, to bomb and strafe the Jap positions." Hozempa then proceeded to provide the Bass family with the information about the search mission for Herbie and Aflred and the likelihood that they had not survived. Hozempa closed, "[l]et's not give up, unless we are notified officially otherwise. We must petition the Lord to be merciful and send them back to us."[145]

The families' prayers were not answered. The Marine Corps confirmed Herbie's death in a letter dated July 5, 1944. It reported that "a wrecked plane contained the remains of an enlisted man, whose identity [that of the gunner] was definitely established by an identification tag, and the unidentified remains of another man, was located in an isolated location. Since the identified remains were those of the man who accompanied your son on his last flight, it must be concluded that the other remains are those of First Lieutenant Bass."

The administrative date of presumed death was June 13, 1944—just days after the successful D-day landings in Normandy—which was the date upon which the discovery of the wrecked plane was received at Marine Corps Headquarters in Washington. The Marine Corps stated that it would do "everything humanly possible" to preserve the remains, and discussed procedures for returning Herbie's personal effects and settling his pay account.

The news set off yet another round of condolences from family and friends. The Commandant of the Marine Corps sent what must have been its standard letter for the death in action of an officer. Lieutenant General A.A.Vandergrift stated:

> There is little I can say to lessen your grief but it is my earnest hope that the knowledge of your son's splendid record in the service and the thought that he nobly gave his life in the performance of his duty may in some measure comfort you in this sad hour.[146]

---

145 See letter dated June 14, 1944 from Alphonse Hozempa to Mrs. Nathan Bass.
146 Letter date July 4, 1944 from A.A.Vandergrift to Nathan Bass.

The local representative from Orangeburg County to the state House of Representatives, A. J. Hydrick, wrote a handwritten letter stating that "the tragedy of this war is that those who make the supreme sacrifice are never to enjoy living in the new world of freedom that their sacrifices make possible."[147] Professor Josiah Morse, from the University of South Carolina, similarly wrote that "[y]our son gave his life for his country and for freedom. He helped to make this a better and finer world for us and future generations to live in."[148]

A month later, the Marine Corps Commandant notified the Bass family that Herbie had been posthumously promoted to the rank of Captain "as a token of the meritorious service of one of our most gallant and faithful Marines." Herbie was awarded the Purple Heart Medal, the Asiatic-Pacific Campaign Medal, and the Victory Medal World War II.[149]

Herbie Bass's effects, including his medals.

---

147 Letter dated July 6, 1944 from A.J. Hydrick to Mr. and Mrs. Bass.
148 Letter dated July 9, 1944 from Josiah Morse to Mr. and Mrs. Nathan Bass.
149 Official service record of Herbert Bass.

It would be another four years, however—in February 1948—before the family was notified that Herbie's remains were en route to the United States for delivery to Dunbar Funeral Home in Columbia. The family published a notice "expressing to friends over the State our deepest appreciation and thanks for their kindness and sympathy to us in the death and burial of our son." The funeral was held at the Hebrew Benevolent Cemetery in Columbia (founded in 1822) with full military honors.

So ended the life of Herbert Bass, a patriotic Jewish-American from North, South Carolina, who'd predicted a long and hard war, "a death struggle for everything that is worthwhile living for." Herbie put it well, at the beginning of the war, when he said that his country would have "been far worse off" if, without the "great sacrifice" of those who would surely die in the coming war, "we should have lost" the war.[150] Herbie's sacrifice made for a better world, one his siblings and their offspring would enjoy.

In honor of Herbie, the American Legion post in North was named after him and the town's other WWII fatality, Manning Nelson—also a Citadel graduate, and son of the town doctor who delivered Ruth. If you drive just past North today on Highway 178 west, you'll pass the Nelson-Bass American Legion Post. If you stop in, you'll see a photo of Herbert Bass and a write-up of his history.

---

150 Letter dated December 13, 1941 from Herbie Bass to Nathan and Esther Bass.

XX. Triumph In Europe

After Herbie's death, both Esther and Nathan became withdrawn, especially Esther, who stopped many of her social activities.

The War went on, of course. Bernie made it home in one piece, surely to the relief of the rest of the family. We don't have any record of how Bernie received the news first that his brother was missing in action, and later declared dead, but it must have hit him hard. Sometime in the spring of 1943, Bernie had a 15-day leave in which he spent time in North and also went up to Lowell, Massachusetts to visit his Uncle Harry and other relatives there. The Lowell newspaper interviewed him and ran an article about his visit and his service, but there was no mention in the article of Herbie.[151] Bernie also spent Thanksgiving 1943 at home in North, enjoying "an excellent meal" with the family and also Miriam and Esther Robin.[152] After Thanksgiving, Bernie and three other members of his squadron holed up at a base in Avon Park, Florida, waiting for orders telling them where they would go next.

In a letter to his Grandmother Rose and Aunt Sadye, Bernie said he was "taking life easy, while waiting for the Army to put me to work." He'd heard that Aunt Sadye was getting married and asked that she be sure to invite him to the wedding as he would save up his leave to attend. Now 25, he also, almost bashfully, told Sadye he had "sort of started looking for a wife" and asked that if she knew "any real nice Jewish girls who are coming down to Florida this winter, tell them to write to your nephew."[153]

---

151 See "Daredevil Yank Fliers Yearn For, of All Things, Milk," Lowell newspaper, date unknown. Bernie told the newspaper a story that when he and some of his fellow fliers returned to Miami after several months overseas, they made a bee-line to a local restaurant where each immediately ordered a quart of fresh milk.
152 See letter dated December 14, 1943 from Bernie Bass to Rose and Sadye Cohn.
153 Id.

Esther Robin Kaminsky with Alan Brody at his bar mitzvah.

Meanwhile, in Poland, Mottl and Goldie Bass were struggling just to survive each day. They and their other two cellar mates had settled into more or less of a "routine"—if you could call living in a tiny hole in the ground for months on end a routine—to get through the days. It wasn't easy. Apart from the physical discomforts, which included going weeks without bathing or cleaning their clothes, there was the constant danger of being discovered by the Germans or by one of the other peasant families living in the village. Discovery would mean death, both for the Jewish refugees in hiding and for their protectors.

Mottl and the others became nocturnal creatures, living in the dark most of the time. Once or twice each day, the trap door would open and Janova, the strong-willed peasant woman who took them in, would hand them down some food. It wasn't much—Janova barely had enough food to feed her own family. At the same time, Mottl or one of the others would hand up the bucket they all had to use as a toilet.

There were other challenges. Worms would come out of the ground. Fleas infested their hole, each one having to be handpicked and killed. Lice got into their hair and clothes. With plenty of time on their hands, Felix Zandman, the teenager hiding with them, found it to be a "constant pastime" to painstakingly remove these creatures.[154]

Between days of absolute boredom there were occasional instances of sheer terror. One day everyone was lying quietly in the hole, thinking their own thoughts, when they heard Janova's foot tapping the signal that Germans were in the house. They heard a dog—not the Puchalski's dog—whining. Surely the German dog would pick up the smell they must have been emitting in their hole. Soon, however, they heard barking in the yard as the two dogs got angry with each other. After awhile, Janova tapped the all clear signal. A German had come in the house, obviously suspicious. Fortunately, Janovoa, seeing him coming with the dog, sprinkled pepper on the floor to confuse the dog's sense of smell. It later turned out that while Mottl and company were hiding, Janova's husband was having an affair with another woman. When he broke it off, she broached her suspicions to the Germans that the Puchalskis might be hiding someone. Thanks to Janova's courage and quick thinking, the German soldier found nothing.

While hiding, Mottl was in charge of keeping the calendar, including figuring out when the Jewish holidays were, to stave off disorientation. "'Aha,' he would say after some arcane calculation, 'tomorrow must be the first day of Pesach. Let's not eat bread'—assuming we had any bread. Or if there was only bread, we'd pretend it was matzoh and talk about it."[155]

---

154 *Never The Last Journey* at 103.
155 *Id.* at 115.

In February 1944, after a year of hiding in the hole, yet another refugee—Esther Shapiro Heidemark—showed up and joined the four already in hiding. She had been hiding in an attic in Grodno until the patriarch of the family hiding her was arrested by the Gestapo for working with the underground. With the discipline the others had already mastered, they were able to accommodate Esther. By that time, the news from the battlefront was more encouraging—the Red Army was on the offensive, less than 350 miles from Grodno.[156]

By June the news was even better—the Americans and British had crossed the English Channel and opened a second front in Europe. By July, the Red Army was approaching Grodno as it steadily beat back the Germans. Yet, as excitement rose in the hole, so did the sense of danger as the battle drew closer. Then one day the Jewish refugees heard cars pulling up outside, followed by German voices. They soon found out that German units were assembling in the area to take a stand as the Red Army came on. Janova said it was too dangerous to open the trap door for food while the Germans were around.

On Sunday, July 16, 1944, after a couple of days of hearing German units coming and going, while the sound of artillery punctuated day and night, the refugees heard all kinds of noises of men and machinery around the house. Soon, German voices were telling the Puchalskis to get out quickly, that the Germans were going to fight right there. Janova and Jan rapped on the trap door and said they would have to go. Jan said something about a goat, and then the house became silent. Later, to their horror, some German troops decided to sleep in the house.

Another day passed, with more fighting. It appeared the Germans had decided to take a stand at the nearby river. With no way to get more food, and in constant fear of being discovered, the refugees made a fateful decision: that night, they would leave. As night came on, another German came and slept on a sofa just across the room from the hole. After he was asleep and snoring, the refugees silently slipped out of their dungeon. As they crossed the village on a moon-lit night, they found themselves in the midst of a battle, with artillery shells screaming through the air and explosions rocking the ground. They'd gone no more than fifty yards when they were stopped by a

---

156 Id. at 118.

German guard. While Mottl was trying, in Polish, to convince a German captain that they were Poles fleeing from the Bolsheviks, Goldie fainted, as they had planned, as if from lack of food. The German, with other things to do, told the whole group to take refuge behind a hill for the night.

The next morning, a German soldier threatened to kill them all, but an officer instead had them sent into some woods where they were examined by an SS officer. The SS man decided that Mottl and Goldie were orientals and that Sender was an Aryan, and ordered them all to get out of the area. If seen again, he promised, they'd be shot. With help from a peasant woman in another village, one whom Goldie had known, the group made their way to a deserted cottage in the woods. They had eaten nothing for days. Fortunately, the next day the peasant woman showed up with a pot of chicken soup.

The battle continued to rage. The following day, Felix went into a village looking for an old friend of his father's in the hope of getting some more food. Instead, he was caught by two German soldiers who demanded his papers. When he told them they were in his house two kilometers away, they decided just to let him go. Later that day, the man Felix had been looking for showed up at their cottage with a loaf of bread and a piece of fatback, which did wonders for the group.

As the battle went on, danger was at every turn. At one point, three German soldiers appeared at the cottage. After a tense moment when one asked whether the refugees were "Juden"—Jews—another said, no, they're clearly Poles. The soldiers promised to return with some food. True to their word, two of them did return, with food and other gifts, but it soon became apparent they were really interested in Goldie. One took Goldie in a room while the other guarded the door, Mottl trembling in anger. A few minutes later, however, they came out, Goldie unmolested—she had begged the soldier not to rape her, invoking his own sisters and mother.

Finally, on the morning of July 24, 1944 the group awoke to silence. The Germans were gone. The Russians had arrived. For Mottl and Goldie Bass and the others who had hidden with them, the war was over.

Martin (Mottl) and Goldie Bass.

XXI. Prosperity And Social Change At Home

With the end of World War II came an economic boom and the beginning of some major changes in the rural South. Millions of troops returned, including many African-Americans who had served honorably and courageously in the military to "keep the world free," only to come home and face state-sanctioned racial discrimination. Harry Truman was President. The Cold War was beginning, but the American economy, fully recovered from the Great Depression by war spending and supplying goods and services to a devastated Europe just beginning to rebuild, was humming.

In North, the loss of Herbie had not gone away. Indeed, at the end of the war, his remains had still not been returned home. His death was probably never far from the minds of Esther and Nathan. The children were growing up. Jack, the youngest, was eleven years old by the time V-J Day arrived in August, 1945.

A year earlier, in a departure for the Bass family and a sign of its economic recovery, Esther sent Jack to Camp Highland Lake, near Hendersonville, N.C., for eight weeks in the summer when he turned ten years old. It was the first time Jack had been separated from his mother, and after she dropped him off he became so homesick that a counselor had to sit with him on a bench beside the lake, consoling him as he sobbed uncontrollably. As is so often the case, however, Jack quickly began enjoying his experience away from home, including exposure to a few other Jewish boys his age. Together, they would cruise the dining hall tables after breakfast, looking for uneaten pieces of bacon, which for them was an exotic food not encountered at home.

The following summer, as the War came to its conclusion, Jack went to Camp Osceola, a Jewish camp for boys from throughout the South, where he was immersed for the first time in an almost totally Jewish environment, with worship services on Friday nights and Saturday mornings. There was no bacon at Camp Osceola. On the second day of camp, Jack got into a fight with another kid, who had been tormenting a pudgy boy with glasses, whose family had fled Germany to escape the Holocaust, by calling him a "dirty little Nazi." Outraged, Jack knocked the tormentor down with a surprise blow to the jaw. Later, they became friends.

Jack Bass towers over his parents in North.

At the other end of the Bass family, Bernie, true to his word to his Aunt Sadye, had found the nice Jewish girl he wanted to marry, Faye Rivkin from Chicago. Bernie met Faye, whose father owned a latex glove manufacturing company, while she was a member of the Coast Guard, and they married in 1944. The following year, after discharge from the Army Air Corps, Bernie enrolled in law school at the University of Michigan. Their first son, Herbert—called Herbie in honor of Bernie's deceased younger brother—was born October 30, 1945. Two years later, another son, Raymond, was born.

After law school, Bernie and family moved to Chicago, where he worked a year or two for his father-in-law at Latex Glove Co. He then reenlisted in what was now the U.S. Air Force and spent much of the next three years at an Air Force base in Savannah, Georgia, where he also taught a Sunday School class at the local temple. Bernie served as the wing legal assistance officer, and as wing claims officer, during his tour of duty, which was with the Second Bombardment Wing. Upon his discharge, Bernie joined the Savannah investment firm of Vanedoe, Chisholm and Co., where he specialized "in servicing the investment accounts of air force personnel."[157]

With African-American veterans returning from the war and demanding equal rights, and with the Truman administration slowly moving toward such greater protections, the old social order in the South began to come under attack. With it came a resurgence of the Ku Klux Klan. One day, Jack noticed some Klan application cards for "white Christian men" on the drug store soda fountain down the street from Nathan's store. He picked one up and took it to his father. Nathan was normally not one to look for trouble, and as a merchant wisely avoided controversy and community conflict.

This time was different. Without hesitation, Nathan walked back to the drug store with Jack beside him, handed the application card to his Masonic Lodge brother, addressed him by name, and asked directly, "Can I join?" The man averted his eyes and said nothing. The incident made an impact on Jack, who usually felt "some distance" from his father: "at that moment I felt a warm glow of respect" for him.

By 1948 racial issues were roiling South Carolina. The state's governor, Strom Thurmond, was running for President on the "Dixiecrat" ticket, representing Southern Democrats who had walked out of the party's national convention over disagreements with Truman and national Democratic party leaders over civil rights issues. In North, the KKK became active. The "grand dragon" of the Ku Klux Klan at the time lived in Leesville, about 25 miles from North. Three times that fall, always on Saturday nights, Klan motorcades drove slowly down the main street of North, passing Nathan's store. The first time, about 40 black people

---

157 "Capt. S. B. Bass Ends Tour of Duty, Air Force Officer To Join Savannah Company," newspaper and date unknown.

huddled in fear at the back of the store. The second time, a similar group came inside the store, watching through the glass doors in front. The third time, they stood in front of the store, their backs next to the display windows.[158]

Despite the upheaval, little changed in North, at least for the time being. Blacks still attended far inferior segregated schools and faced discrimination in most aspects of their lives. Until an order that year by U.S. District Judge J. Waities Waring, no blacks in South Carolina could vote in the white Democratic primaries that decided elections in the one-party South of the era. There were no African-American public officials in North, in Orangeburg County, or anywhere in the state. Nathan refused to be intimidated by the Klan activity, and he continued to derive much of his business from the black community in and around North.

Jews in the South at the time tended to be more sympathetic to the struggle for civil rights than other whites, although less liberal than their Jewish counterparts from northern states. Part of this was simply experience. "[T]he Jewish immigrant had never seen black men before; he was more willing to respond out of actual experience with the Negro than out of a twisted history of slavery, guilt, and pathological hate. When the Negro smiled at the Jew, the Jew smiled back."[159]

At the same time, many Jews preferred simply not to get involved in the civil rights issue, which was volatile and potentially bad for business. Eli Evans quotes one rabbi who served in the South for many years: "Sure, there are some biased people, but by and large, Jews are sympathetic. They just don't want to stick their necks out."[160]

Nathan also still had his eye on foreign affairs, particularly as they affected Jews. A supporter of establishing a Jewish state in Palestine, Nathan wrote a letter to the editor of his local newspaper—the Orange-

---

158 Many years later, as a reporter, Jack interviewed and wrote about some Klansmen. He found that they were usually quite poor, barely educated, and with so little self-esteem that membership in the KKK provided a sense of belonging and status that otherwise was lacking in their lives.

159 Evans, *The Provincials*, at 276.

160 *Id.* at 275. The rabbi told a joke about an all-Jewish jury accidentally selected for a civil rights trial. "When the judge asked the foreman for his verdict, the foreman announced, 'Your honor, we've decided not to get involved!'"

burg *Times & Democrat*—in February 1947, responding to an editorial headed "British Problem in Palestine." The editorial concluded with a sentence reading, "It is difficult to cope with the gangster methods"— evidently referring to raids on British targets by the Jewish resistance in Palestine.

Nathan started out on a personal note: "Now, Mr. Editor, knowing you personally as good as I do, I feel that you didn't mean any harm, as I personally don't approve the methods the Terrorists are using."[161] Nathan then went on to explain a bit of history, including numerous promises by the British that Jews would be allowed to establish a homeland in Palestine. He then asked, "What would you suggest for them [the Jews now in Palestine or trying to get in] to do?" "The reason of writing," Nathan continued, "is first as a Jew who is fortunate to be an American Jew, and, second, as a good American citizen who would love to see Justice done."

Getting back the ongoing violence in Palestine, Nathan asked, "If someone took away your great-grandfather's estate and the court would revise generations later that the estate belongs to you and would tell you to return and after you return, they would stop you, would you fight for your rights?" Nathan closed by reciting to the editor some lines that had appeared right below the editorial on the Palestine problem: "Right below your British problem you have a few lines there which says, 'A nation which is unwilling to fight for its existence will not have a long existence,' and 'Peace is ideal but it is never to be purchased by abject surrender of fundamental rights.'"

Nathan wasn't yet done helping the Jews of Europe to find a place they could call home.

---

161 Letter To Editor, *Times & Democrat*, February 1947. Ironically, given today's emphasis on "Arab terrorism," Nathan's reference to the "Terrorists" was aimed at armed Jewish groups that were fighting an underground campaign for independence of a Jewish state at that time.

XXII. Martin And Goldie Come To America

In 1948, with help from Nathan and his brother Harry, Mottl—now Martin—and Goldie Bass came to America. They settled in Atlanta, Georgia, where they operated a small grocery store for many years. The road to America for Martin and Goldie was not an easy one, although certainly much better than their eighteen months hiding in a dirty hole in Poland.

After the Russians swept the Germans away in July 1944, Martin and Goldie returned to Grodno. Upon entering the town, they were arrested by Soviet soldiers—they had no identification papers of any kind—and taken to the Grodno prison. There, a sympathetic Russian soldier who was also Jewish apologized and set them free. Over the next couple of days, other Jews who had survived and emerged from their hiding places began returning to Grodno. As Felix Zandman tells it, "When we saw each other we embraced and wept, none of us able to keep down our emotions. We all wanted to know what had happened, to hear about the others, and to tell the story of our own horrors and miracles."[162]

The Basses' savior, Janova Puchalski, showed up in Grodno a few days later, delighted to hear that all had survived. After the Germans left, the Puchalskis had returned to their home, only to find the cellar empty. They had feared the worst, so were relieved to find their charges alive, safe and relatively free in Grodno.

Within a couple of months, Mottl and Goldie moved to Bialystok (where Esther Cohen Bass was born), on the first step of a journey they hoped would take them to Israel. While they never got to Israel, they did help others, their apartment in Bialystok becoming a sort of way station for Jews seeking to resettle in Israel or other parts of the west. As Zandman, who stayed there himself, put it, the Basses' house "didn't appear on any map, but people coming through on all sorts of business knew about it. Partisans stopped in, organizers for Aliyah Bet (the

---

162 *Never The Last Journey* at 138.

illegal immigration to Palestine), gun runners for the Haganah (Palestine's underground Jewish army), refugees of all sorts. They knew the house and stayed there when they came through the city."[163]

In March, 1945, with the war in Europe all but over, Mottl and Goldie "left Bialystok for Lublin, where the Bricha—the chief organization that smuggled Jews out of Europe to Palestine—ran one of its main operations."[164] Mottl even arranged for Felix Zandman to join a group of young people about to be smuggled into Palestine with some kibbutzniks, but a friend arrived and persuaded Zandman to wait so he could help his uncle Sender, who had gotten in trouble with Soviet authorities.

Neither Zandman nor Mottl and Goldie ended up in Palestine, however. In 1948, the Basses, with help from their uncles Nathan and Harry in the United States, emigrated to America. Zandman took a more circuitous route, first spending a number of years in France, receiving his PhD. in physics, before emigrating to the U.S. in 1956, where he founded an electronics company, Vishay, that went on to become a Fortune 500 corporation listed on the New York Stock Exchange.

They didn't forget the Pulchalskis, the Polish peasant family who risked their lives to save five Jewish refugees. In June 1987, Felix Zandman arranged a ceremony at Yad Vashem—the Jewish Holocaust Memorial in Jerusalem—in honor of Jan and Janova Pulchalski and their family. Jan and Janova had passed away by then, but their children—whose lives were put at risk as well—were still living. As part of the ceremony, a tree was planted in the small forest outside the memorial building, commemorating the Puchalskis as "righteous persons" who had saved Jewish lives.[165]

After settling in Atlanta, Martin and Goldie Bass followed the footsteps of many of their Jewish émigré forebears, starting a family and settling into American life much like Nathan had generations earlier. They had two children, Noah and Marian. Noah became a physician in Pittsburgh, Pennsylvania, where he married and raised his own family.

Marian recalled a lesson she learned from her father that just as easily could've been one Nathan taught his children. When Marian was in

---

163 *Id.* at 152.
164 *Id.* at 154-55.
165 *See Never The Last Journey* at 396-400.

high school, her history teacher assigned "Masters of Deceit," an anti-Communist tract written by FBI director J. Edgar Hoover. Martin was no Communist sympathizer, but he believed his daughter should have balance in her education. He told her to read "The Communist Manifesto," by Karl Marx. "After I had finished both books," said Marian, "my father and I had a long conversation about both, in which he helped me to refine my understanding of the books, of the world, of politics and of what it takes to be truly educated."[166]

Martin also had a brother, Michel, who had escaped Grodno just in time, making it to London, where he spent the rest of the war. Michel, too, came to America, settling in New Jersey with his wife, Risa (Reisl) Tabak. Their daughter Ellen became a lawyer and lives in New Jersey with her family.

After Goldie passed away, Martin moved to Pittsburgh to be near his son. Martin passed away in 2002, and his brother Michel passed away in 2009.

Michel Bass.

---

166 Letter to the Editor, *New York Times*, Feb. 16, 2009.

XXIII. The Bass Sisters Leave Home

The four Bass sisters—Ruth, Frances, Marcia and Lucille—were always close to each other. Growing up, the four of them slept in two double beds in the middle bedroom of the house in North—Ruth and Marcia in one bed, Frances and Lucille in the other, snuggling to keep warm. As they matured and graduated from North High School, the girls went out into the world and followed their own paths. Yet they managed to stay close to each other even as they went their separate ways.

After years of helping out in their daddy's store, the girls, all of whom went on to college, swore they wouldn't be in retail sales. Yet two of them, Frances and Lucille, ended up running clothing stores with their husbands in small towns, just like their parents had done in North. Three of them stayed in South Carolina—never too far from North. And all of them followed their parents' wishes to marry Jewish men, despite growing up in a town where they were the only Jewish family. As Marcia put it, "because we were the only Jewish family in North, we all had a late social life because Daddy wouldn't let us go out with non-Jewish boys."

Ruth, the oldest, graduated from the University of South Carolina in 1943 with a two-year Secretarial Science Certificate. She went to work for the State Board of Health in Columbia. While working in Columbia, she met Isaac Jacobs, a devout Orthodox Jew. It turned out this wasn't just a chance meeting—instead it was orchestrated through the network of itinerant Jewish salesmen in South Carolina, with Ruth's mom, Esther, serving as matchmaker from afar, not unlike Jewish traditions in the old country.

At the time, Isaac was working as a traveling salesman in his family business, Jacobs Hosiery Co. in Charleston—and his territory included much of South Carolina and part of North Carolina. He was familiar to Nathan and Esther. One of Isaac's sales partners, Seymour Some, would also come through North periodically, and on one of his stops, at some point in 1948, Esther mentioned that she had some daughters living in

Columbia and asked about Isaac. Seymour mentioned the conversation to Isaac and next thing he knew Isaac was dating Ruth.

It took awhile for the relationship to blossom, however. Next time Seymour was in North, Esther started asking him what had happened with Isaac and Ruth because they were no longer seeing each other. That was news to Seymour. In June 1950, however, Isaac called on some T-shirt businesses in Myrtle Beach with whom he'd done business before (they were owned by Sephardic Jews), then drove to a hotel where the S.C. Department of Public Health was having a convention. Ruth, who worked for the department as a secretary, was attending the convention and they met again. During the following months Isaac corresponded with Ruth and expressed his affection for her.[167]

In March 1951 Seymour left Jacobs Hosiery to go into business with his father and brother in New Jersey. A couple months later, when he drove down to South Carolina to get his wife (Betty), he learned that Isaac and Ruth were back together and getting married. Isaac had bought a diamond ring, and while sitting in a parked car near the runway at North Air Force Base he proposed to her. On June 17, 1951, Ruth and Isaac were married at the House of Peace Synagogue in Columbia, with Seymour and Betty, and others, in attendance. Ruth was 28 years old, Isaac 35. They soon moved to Charleston, where Jacobs Hosiery was located.

---

167 See Tzvi Jacobs, "Diamonds in the Sand," The Jewish Press online, http://www. jewishpress.com/pageroute.do/32816/ (accessed 12/19/10).

Wedding of Ruth Bass and Isaac Jacobs, June 1951. From left to right, standing: Gussie Stotsky, Marcia Bass Brody, Arthur Ginsberg, Harry Bass, Anne Bass, Nathan Bass, Ruth Bass Jacobs, Isaac Jacobs, Esther Bass, Jack Bass, Estelle Lury, Myer Lury, Lucille Bass Lipsitz and Nathan Stotsky. Seated: Frances Bass Ginsberg, Ida Bass Robin, Sadye Cohen Green, Fanny Cohen Slomin.

Ruth wasn't the first of the Bass girls to the altar, however. Frances, the next oldest, was always popular and gregarious, getting along with just about anyone. "When she walks into a room, the interior lights up and you can feel her presence. She arrives with a smile on her face and cheery upbeat outlook in her conversation. With Frances the glass is always half full and if she's dealt a lemon she'll make lemonade. She can find magic in a blue sky or the twinkling stars at night. If there is a death, a newborn baby, new neighbors or an illness, Frances is always the first one at the doorstep with a homemade cake, fruit cobbler, or meal."[168]

Frances earned an associate degree in Secretarial Science in 1944 after two years at the University of South Carolina. After that she worked at various jobs in Columbia, including the Columbia Army Air Corps Base, the State Board of Health, and Mutual Benefit Insurance Co. Frances paid rent to and lived with her good friend Judy Sunshine, another young Jewish woman in Columbia, and Judy's husband Jeff. One day, while employed at Mutual Benefit, Frances met Arthur

168 Character sketch of Frances Bass Ginsburg by Marcia Bass Brody.

Ginsburg on a blind date. Arthur had just opened a shoe department at his brother's store in Bishopville and worked part-time for a National Guard unit as a sergeant. Judy urged Frances to "hook on to" Arthur as the "nicest, cutest boy" she had dated since being in Columbia. Frances followed that advice, marrying Arthur in 1949 after just six months of courtship.

Frances joined Arthur and his brother Howard in managing Ginsberg's Ladies Shop in the town of Bishopville, South Carolina (population 3,500), county seat of rural Lee County, about 80 miles northeast of North. Bishopville had its own rich Jewish history. "In 1927, this dot on the South Carolina map was home to 93 Jewish individuals, earning the town a place on the American Jewish Committee's list of 871 independent Jewish communities in the United States."[169] It wasn't long before Frances was a fixture in the store, which had a surprisingly fashionable line of ladies' clothing for such a small town. After a few years, Howard moved to Charleston, leaving the store entirely in the hands of Frances and Arthur. For years, people came from miles around to shop at Ginsberg's, perhaps attracted by the store's famous slogan, initiated by Arthur's father Sam: "If your clothes are not becoming to you, then you'd better be coming to us."

Marcia Bass, the third oldest daughter, proved to be quite independent. After graduating from a senior class of nine students at North High School, Marcia followed her sisters to the University of South Carolina in Columbia. She graduated in January, 1948 with a B.S. degree in business administration. After graduating, Marcia was in her father's store one day when a salesman stopped by. He happened to have with him a newspaper from Charlotte, North Carolina. Although Charlotte was less than 150 miles away, Marcia knew nothing of the city. Nonetheless, she answered an ad in the newspaper for a secretarial position, got called in for an interview, and was hired for the job.

That fall, Marcia asked for time off to observe Rosh Hashanah and Yom Kippur. Many years later, while having lunch with her former boss on a stopover in Charlotte, Marcia learned that the firm's policy in 1948

---

169 See "Yiddeshkeyt" in Bishopville," The Jewish Historical Society of South Carolina, Vol. XIV, No. 1 (Spring 2009) http://www.jhssc.org/2009_Spring_JHSSC_Newsletter. pdf (accessed 11/11/2009). By 2009 there were only two Jews left in Bishopville, one of them being Frances.

had been not to employ Jews, but that they hadn't known she was Jewish until she asked for and was given leave for the High Holy Days. The firm kept her on—she continued there for another eight years.

While living in Charlotte, Marcia tried to attend services on Saturdays at the local conservative synagogue, hitchhiking at times because she did not have a car. Whenever a single Jewish man moved into the area, the rabbi would give Marcia his name. One of those men was Hy Brody, hired by the synagogue as its executive director in 1953. Marcia and Hy hit it off. By the next summer, on June 27, 1954, they were married. The wedding took place in Columbia, with Rabbi Karesh of the House of Peace Synagogue presiding. It was a colorful wedding: there was a florist convention in town at the time, and Esther persuaded the florists to donate flowers for the wedding and chupah.

Marcia and Hy returned to Charlotte, where their first child, Roslyn, was born in September, 1955. While in Charlotte, the local Hadassah chapter offered Marcia a one month scholarship to a "Brandeis camp" session in North Carolina.[170] Marcia could only get two weeks of paid vacation from her job, so she decided to go for two weeks. She liked it so much—the camp was like living on a kibbutz in Israel—that she called her office and asked if she could take two more weeks, unpaid. They not only let her take the additional two weeks, but they paid for it.

Marcia's new family didn't stay long in Charlotte, however. The synagogue did not renew Hy's contract, so they moved to Philadelphia, where Hy was born and raised. A non-stop talker and "born salesman" who could "sell ice to eskimos," Hy accepted a job as a professional fundraiser for the Jewish National Fund, which had him traveling most of the time. He later took a job as the Executive Director for the Philadelphia chapter of the American Technion Society, where he worked for 20 years. After moving to Philadelphia, Marcia had two more children, Alan and Neal. While Hy worked, Marcia

---

170 The Brandeis Camp Institute was named for Justice Louis Brandeis, first Jewish Supreme Court Justice in the U.S., and was intended to combat assimilation of young U.S. Jews by making "the great ethical heritage of Judaism" relevant to them. The institute continues to this day on a large piece of land outside Los Angeles. See American Jewish University, History, at: http://www.ajula.edu/content/contentunit. asp?CID=141&u=5257t=0 (accessed November 5, 2009).

stayed at home, raising her family, and occasionally making visits to South Carolina to see her parents and siblings.

Marcia never forgot what Hadassah had done for her in Charlotte, however, and after moving to Philadelphia she felt she should pay the organization back by becoming an active member. Over the years she held just about every office in the Hanna Senesch chapter, including serving as its president for two years.

Lucille, the youngest of the four sisters, attended Winthrop College in Rock Hill, S.C., where she earned a B.A. degree in sociology after four years of study. While in college, Lucille "thought of Mama and Daddy having plenty of money." She would write checks for whatever she needed on the Bass Mercantile Co. account—if there wasn't enough money to cover the check, her father would be notified by the bank and add enough to cover it. "When I got married," said Lucille, "Mama told me that she and Daddy just finished paying off their last debt—they borrowed money to send us all through college."

Lucille liked to drive, and during both high school and college she would frequently drive her parents to Savannah and Augusta, Georgia, cities that bordered South Carolina, where Nathan and Esther would visit wholesalers to purchase goods for their store.[171]

After college, Lucille worked in Georgetown, S.C.—on the coast between Charleston and Myrtle Beach—as a caseworker for the Department of Public Welfare. She lived with the Jewish Rosen family, which included the town's sixth Jewish mayor, Sylvan Rosen, and his brother Meyer, who later won election as a state legislator. Lucille then took a year of graduate courses in social work at the University of South Carolina in Columbia. After that, she took a job with the Department of Public Welfare in Charleston.

There she met Joe Lipsitz, who she married in January 1955. They settled in Beaufort, S.C.—on the lower coast of the state—where Joe was born and raised. Joe and Lucille had some things in common: Joe's Jewish immigrant father settled in Beaufort in 1902 and established

---

171 Lucille recalls that her father would go to Rubin's Wholesale in Columbia just about every week, with additional trips to wholesalers in Charleston, Augusta and Savannah when needed, and at least one buying trip to New York every year. Salesmen would also come by the store regularly.

Lipsitz Department store on Bay Street, the town's historic retail center. Joe and his sister Ethel had operated the store for a number of years, and continued to do so after Lucille settled with Joe in Beaufort.

Like her sisters, Lucille promptly started a family. Her first child, Sandra, was born in November, 1955. Barry, Neil and Judy followed. As the children grew older, Lucille became more and more involved in the family store, finally working full-time after Ethel retired.

Although the four sisters who had once shared one room and two beds together were now scattered about with their own families to tend to, they remained close, getting together frequently—sometimes in North, sometimes at each other's homes—and keeping up with each other via mail and telephone. They retained their sibling bond of friendship as each pursued her own life in the world.

The Bass sisters.

XXIV. The Youngest Son

When WWII ended, Nathan's youngest son, Jack, was only 11 years old. Jack enjoyed sports, playing baseball, basketball and football at North High School. He also followed sports in the news, reading the sports sections of three newspapers, as well as subscribing to the weekly baseball publication, *The Sporting News*. Jack was interested in journalism and wanted to be a sports writer. While serving as official scorer for North's semipro baseball team, Jack also worked as a sports "stringer" for three newspapers, calling in the results of baseball games for publication. Once, he called the *Columbia Record* to report on a fire at North School—that afternoon the story was on page one, and Jack later received a check for two dollars for his trouble. Another time, he sent an item in for a column in the monthly *Sport* magazine and earned $15 when it ran.

Jack followed in the footsteps of his siblings, going to college at the University of South Carolina. There, he nurtured his interest in journalism, despite the discouraging words he'd heard from the editor of the Orangeburg newspaper the summer before starting college. He became editor of "The Gamecock," the school newspaper, and worked as a sports reporter during two summers for the Charleston *News and Courier,* staying with Ruth as her family was getting started in the mid-'50's. Jack also met his future wife, Carolyn McClung, through journalism, who succeeded him as editor of The Gamecock following a semester as his managing editor.

When Jack graduated from "Carolina," the university noted with pride that he was the sixth member of his family to attend the school. Columbia's morning newspaper, *The State*, deemed it newsworthy enough to run a photo of the entire Bass family, taken at Jack's graduation, the next day. Following his graduation, Jack and a friend from North—John William Reed—took off on a 7,500 mile road trip, in Jack's new Volkswagen with its engine in the rear and gas tank under the hood, visiting the Grand Canyon, Yellowstone, and Yosemite along the way.

Jack's graduation from the University of South Carolina.

Upon his return, Jack reported to Newport, Rhode Island for Navy Officer Candidate School. Like his brothers, Jack wanted to fly. He became a Navy flight officer, serving as an airborne early warning specialist on an AD5W—a single engine propeller driven converted dive bomber used for anti-submarine patrols. These ungainly looking planes, with a large radar in the belly that made them appear pregnant, looked like they would never be able to take off and land from the tiny deck of an aircraft carrier, but Jack survived three and half years of active duty in the Navy. He served another 16 and a half years as navigator and tactical coordinator in the Navy Reserve, flying in land-based twin-propeller anti-submarine planes with a crew of ten.

Two months after his commission as an ensign, Jack married Carolyn McClung, his fellow *Gamecock* editor. While all of Jack's other surviving siblings married Jewish spouses, Jack's mate was a statuesque red-headed Presbyterian from Lexington, Virginia. All of their parents had reservations about a mixed marriage, but Esther attended the wedding with Ruth, while Nathan was too ill to attend. Carolyn's Presbyterian minister conducted the wedding ceremony, but agreed to omit any references to "Jesus."

Jack and Carolyn had three children. Ken, born in November 1958 in Carolyn's hometown of Lexington while Jack was temporarily stationed in the Philippines, was given the middle name Nathan in honor of his grandfather who had passed away at the beginning of the year. David was born a year later in California, while Jack was stationed at North Island Naval Air Station in Coronado, across the bay from San Diego. Elizabeth was born four years later in Columbia.

Both of Jack's boys had a bris (circumcision ceremony) presided over by a rabbi, and Elizabeth as an infant went through the traditional Jewish naming ceremony. Before their marriage, the couple had met with Episcopal Bishop James A. Pike of New York, who had written about acceptance of interfaith marriages. After reading a newspaper article about a young man raised as a Christian who had been denied membership in an exclusive country club because his father was Jewish, Jack insisted the children be brought up Jewish. Carolyn acceded, to the chagrin of her parents. Jack's family regularly visited Carolyn's parents in Lexington over the Christmas holidays, giving the children exposure to both their parents' religions.

XXV. Grandchildren

As the Bass family moved into the prosperous 1950's, Nathan and Esther's home began filling with grandchildren. Bernie got it started with his two boys, Herbie and Raymond. Growing up in Chicago, Bernie's boys must have been fascinated by the trips to see their grandparents in North (which they also visited when Bernie was stationed in Savannah on his second Air Force tour).

Herbie Bass fondly recalls those trips. "Grandpa would always take us to the store and show us off to his friends and customers as his two oldest grandchildren. He would let us play with the cash register and act as though we were the sales clerks." Like all Bass grandchildren, they would also harvest pecans from the large pecan trees growing in Nathan and Esther's backyard, learning how to crack open the nuts and enjoy their moist sweetness while sitting on the back steps or the porch. As Herbie and Raymond grew older, they learned they had a responsibility as the oldest of what would eventually be 21 cousins. As Herbie recalled, "we would play with them, but we had to be careful and watch over them since we were the oldest."

Ruth's oldest child, Susan, born in 1952, also remembered going to Bass Mercantile Co., which seemed to be the largest store in North. "Lots of black people would hang out in front of the store and be friendly towards Grandpa. It seemed that everyone respected Grandpa Bass." Nathan and Esther still spoke Yiddish around the grandchildren, who thought it was a secret language. Susan recalled Nathan as he was in the 1950's: "He was short, had white hair and used to smoke a lot. I also remember he liked playing cards and always had lots of poker chips. I seem to recall that he was a serious person. He had some old books written in Yiddish in front of the house. I used to wonder how anyone could read them." Susan also admired her grandpa for his ability to fix things around the house and for being a "math wizard" who "could figure out numbers and money faster than any machine."

**Grandma Esther and some of her many
grandchildren at the Bass family home in North.**

One of Ruth's children, Tzvi (born Herbert Jacobs, he changed his name to Tzvi as an adult) recalled visiting the Bass family homestead as a child. Grandma Bass "loved to make us freezer cookies ... she'd cut them and lay them on the cookie tray. They were delicious." He also recalled his grandmother, who "gave only kindness" to her grandchildren, had an old ice cream churn on her back porch. "The flab under her arm shook with the large machine. That was grandma, sweet like ice cream."

Just like her mother, Ruth went on to have seven children: Susan, Tzvi, Charles (who, tragically, died young, in his early 30's), twins Naomi and Sharon, Sarah, and Diane. As Marcia joked about Ruth, "Math was one of her worst subjects, but after she married, she sure learned to multiply."

The rest of Nathan and Esther's offspring all contributed multiple grandchildren to the mix. Frances had three girls—Nancy, Beverly, and Sally—who all grew up in Bishopville with plenty of nice clothes from Ginsberg's Ladies Shop. Marcia's three children—Roslyn, Alan and Neal—grew up in Cheltenham, a township outside Philadelphia. Lucille, raising her family in Beaufort, had four children—Sandra, Barry, Neil, and Judy. Finally, Jack, settling in Columbia after a stint in the Navy and selling his weekly newspaper in suburban Charleston, raised three children as well—Ken, David, and Liz.

The grandchildren were frequent fixtures in the Bass home in North, part of a large, loving family that frequently gathered together for special occasions. Unfortunately, Nathan didn't get the chance to see all his grandchildren, and their time with him was limited. But all of them had time with their grandmother Esther. Esther would teach card games to her grandchildren, and play with them when they were young. The little ones she would have sit on her foot, which she would elevate to give them a ride. Or she would play a game of reflexes. As David described it, "One of us [grandchildren] would place our hands on top of hers and she would try to pull her hand out from under very quickly and touch our hand before we could pull away. Then we would trade positions and try to get her back."

Esther also taught Jack's wife, Carolyn, who wasn't Jewish, how to make excellent potato latkes—a special Chanukah treat.

XXVI. End Of An Era

It was New Year's Day, 1958. Dwight Eisenhower was President and the nation was prospering, despite the Cold War and the Soviet threat. Times were good.

But in the small town of North, it was no day to celebrate. One of the town's leading citizens, Nathan Bass, passed away that day. At age 72, and less than a year after a severe heart attack, a lifetime of smoking cigarettes likely caught up with Nathan as he died of a stroke. Only a few months earlier, Nathan and Esther had celebrated their 40th wedding anniversary.[172]

People from all walks of life stopped by the Bass home on that chilly day, and the next, to pay their respects. The funeral was the next day, at Dunbar Funeral Home, followed by burial at the Hebrew Benevolent Society cemetery where Herbie had been interred. Both of Columbia's rabbis, from the Tree of Life Temple and the House of Peace Synagogue, presided over the service. Nathan's sister Ida and his cousin Nathan Stotsky managed to make it to the funeral. Several prominent members of the local Jewish community served as pallbearers, including Isadore Bernstein, Sam Rubin, Jeff Sunshine, Morris Savitz, Sam Savitz and Arnold Levinson. The members of North Lodge No. 119 of the Masons also served as honorary pallbearers, and Masonic rites were rendered at the grave.[173] Well over 100 mourners signed the register of visitors at the funeral home, many easily recognizable as names from North (Livingstons, Reeds, Cullers) and from the Jewish community throughout South Carolina.[174]

---

172 Victor and Ida Robin contributed $25 to The Day—Jewish Journal in honor of the anniversary. See letter dated Aug. 7, 1957 from Mr. & Mrs. N. Bass to The Day— Jewish Journal, correcting the name of the contributors.

173 See "Nathan Bass, Merchant of North, Dies," The State, Jan. 2, 1958.

174 See In Memoriam book for Nathan Bass.

Nathan Bass, right, with brother Harry and sister Ida.

Contributions in Nathan's memory came in from all over, including donations to the Orangeburg County Methodist Home for the Aged, the Jewish Children's Home in Atlanta, the South Carolina Crippled Children's Society (his favorite charity), the National Heart Association, Blue Baby Research and other worthy institutions.

Nathan's widow, Esther, received hundreds of letters and telegrams of condolence from the rich and the poor, from the Jew and the non-Jew, the prominent and the obscure. The Eastern Star chapter from North—the women's affiliate of the Masons—furnished a complete dinner when the large family returned from the funeral in Columbia. Over the next two weeks the Bass home was filled with cakes, pies, rice, sweet potato casserole, and other dishes brought over by friends, neighbors, and admirers.

It was said that if Diogenes had met Nathan, he would have stopped looking for an honest man. One could walk around North and never hear a bad word uttered about him. Nathan Bass came over from Eastern Europe as a poor, skinny, short Jewish teenager. He was never materially rich by the standards of the time, but he lived a rich life, raising a large family and sending all seven of his children to college so that they could have the things of which he could only dream.

Esther outlived Nathan by many years, not all of them good. For ten years she ran the store by herself, paying the bills and buying the merchandise. She couldn't drive, so she walked to the store every day. In 1968, a decade after Nathan's death, with all of the children grown and well into families of their own, Esther finally decided to close the store, sell the home in North and move to Bishopville, where Frances was living. Esther had a small apartment just down the street, but as she grew older she slipped into the dementia of Alzheimer's disease, to the point she would no longer recognize her own children, who still visited and loved her at a nursing facility two blocks from Frances's home.

In January 1969 the Mayor and Town Council of North thanked Esther for a gift she had given to the town. "I hope some day soon you will journey over here and let us thank you in person. Knowing how much interest you and Mr. Bass always had in Community affairs I am sure you would be pleased with the progress we have made."[175]

---

175 Letter dated Jan. 23, 1969 from Miriam Egleston to Mrs. Esther Bass.

Esther with daughters Marcia, Ruth and Frances in Frances' front yard in Bishopville, S.C.

On May 5, 1974, Esther passed away, at the age of 84, in a local hospital room, with Jack there hearing her final breath. Although she hadn't lived in North for many years, a group of friends and admirers from the town drove to Columbia for the funeral. Esther was buried next to her beloved Nathan in Columbia at the Hebrew Benevolent Society cemetery, in a wooden casket with a Star of David carved on its top. Six of Esther's grandchildren served as pallbearers.

A former Mayor of North, M.E. "Mutt" Livingston, had fond memories of Nathan and Esther. They "were honorable and respected citizens of North. They operated a successful business and contributed unselfish time and money to the welfare of the Town of North and surrounding areas."[176]

As for Bass Mercantile, it is unlikely that it would have survived into the era of the modern South. The main street stores of many small towns have struggled as corporate chains of retail stores, especially

---

176 Letter dated July 26, 1986 from M.E. Livingston to Ruth Jacobs.

Walmart in the larger towns, have come to dominate the landscape, while rural populations have declined as farm children left to experience life in bigger cities with greater opportunity.

Eli Evans relates that even as far back as the early 1970's, when he began researching his book on Southern Jews, the small town Jew store was dying out. "[W]hen I was traveling and interviewing and writing this book, one often heard Jews talk about the dying South. The era of the small-town stores was coming to an end as the proliferation of shopping centers and discount chains abolished the uniqueness of each locale. In the words of one former peddler who had climbed the ladder to become a small-store owner, 'Now every town looks alike.'"[177] Since the 1970's, the trend has only accelerated: "[T]he small-town era that molded so much of the culture of Southern Jews in the twentieth century is vanishing, as the Jews follow the rest of America to the cities and suburbs."[178]

In that regard, Nathan and Esther's children, and especially their grandchildren, followed the trend.

Bass Family Reunion, Columbia, SC, May, 1997. Some, but not all, direct descendants of Nathan and Esther Bass.

177 Evans, The Provincials, at 298. Evans could have added that the social changes in the South, particularly desegregation, also had an impact, as blacks in the South were welcomed to shop in those national chain stores, and so did not have to depend on their friendly local Jewish merchant as before.
178 Evans, The Provincials, at 360. Evans relates that even when he started research on his book back in the early 1970's, the era of small town Jewish merchants was coming to a close

Bass cemetery plot at the Hebrew Benevolent Society Cemetery in Columbia, SC. Nathan, Esther and Herbie are buried here.

XXVII. The Legacy Lives On

Nathan's children did prosper while leading modest but productive lives.

After finishing his stint with the Air Force in 1952, Bernie opened a law practice in Faye's hometown of Chicago. Bernie supported the Chicago Democratic political machine as precinct captain of the city's extensively Jewish 48th Ward. He also indulged his passion for cards, becoming a champion bridge player, a Life Master who played in tournaments, sometimes for cash.

For Jack's children—and probably others of their cousins—Uncle Bernie from the big city of Chicago seemed quite sophisticated. On one visit to Columbia, Bernie explained to Jack's boys how the stock market worked. The entrepreneurial boys immediately went out and started a neighborhood popcorn company, offering shares to the other children on their street. On another trip, Bernie taught Jack's sons how to play bridge, and on a later trip even took Jack's son Ken to a local bridge tournament as his partner.

The Bass siblings, minus Herbie.

Later in life, Bernie worked in a number of positions with the city and county government, eventually retiring as a lawyer in the Cook County Highway Department. He developed Parkinson's disease, and in 1985 he died at the age of 67 of a heart attack suffered as he completed a morning swim.

Ruth, who had always been the most observant of the Bass children, established a kosher, Orthodox home. She worked in the office of the Charleston Hebrew Institute and Brith Shalom-Beth Israel Synagogue as a part time secretary while raising her seven children. She was active in her synagogue's sisterhood, edited the religious school's newsletter and served on the board of the South Carolina Jewish Historical Society. All of Ruth's children continued to be observant Orthodox Jews, and all but Charles (who died young) married and had children—39 in all, many of whom are also grown, married and with children, such that Ruth spent a good deal of her time later in life traveling for births, bar mitzvahs, weddings and other occasions, making at least one visit annually to each of her children.

Ruth's husband, Isaac, passed away on February 21, 1999. Ruth remained active in her synagogue and worked as a volunteer with the Jewish Heritage Collection at the College of Charleston—a special collection at the College's Addlestone Library that houses memorabilia and stories of South Carolina Jews and Jewish life.

Jacobs family (1978). Sitting: Isaac, Ruth, Susan (holding Yaelle), and Michael. Standing: Herbie (Tzvi), Naomi, Sarah, Sharon, Charles, and Dianne.

In April 2004 Ruth was honored as a "Woman Who Makes A Difference" by her synagogue. The rabbi's wife, Barbara Radinsky, gave a speech in Ruth's honor, which tells a lot about the character Ruth developed growing up in an observant Jewish family in a small southern town. After noting Ruth's background, including her relationship to a famous Zionist—her uncle Noah—who died in the Holocaust, Radinsky praised Ruth for her values:

"Ruth was raised in the small southern town of North, the same town that the famous Eartha Kitt came from. Though many southerners were so full of prejudice, Ruth is the epitome of tolerance for one and all no matter the color, the religion, the class, etc. In fact, Ruth is one of the most tolerant, non-judgmental people that I have ever met....

Ruth is an observant Jewish woman who models the integration of ritual and ethical commandments. If someone needs a ride to the doctor, Ruth makes herself available. If someone needs a lift to the drug store, Ruth is there. If someone needs long-term housing or a place for a few days, Ruth opens her home so graciously to those she knows and to strangers as well. We receive phone calls on a weekly basis from travelers who are looking for Shabbat home hospitality. When we ask Ruth to consider hosting these guests that we personally are not always able to accommodate, she rarely refuses. Ruth is the epitome of humility and tolerance, of giving of herself with a full heart, of Hachnosat Orchim (of welcoming visitors), of being a devoted friend and relative, of serving Brith Sholom Beth Israel Congregation and the broader community. The world is a much better place because of Ruth Jacobs. The world would be a much better place if there were more people like Ruth.

The Rabbis say: Al Shloshah Dvorim Haolom Omed, al Hatorah, Al HaAvodah Val Gmilut Chassadim. The world rests on three concepts: On the Torah, on service to God and on acts of loving-kindness. Ruth Bass Jacobs exemplifies these three pillars of Judaism."

Ruth passed away on August 9, 2007, after a brief battle with pancreatic cancer.

Frances still lives in Bishopville, where she is an honored and leading citizen. Her husband, Arthur, called Frances "Babe," a name that stuck, especially after Arthur put a personalized license plate saying "BABE" on her car, ever after called the "Babe mobile." Frances was always busy. Her mother-in-law came to live with them in Bishopville, and later her own mother—Esther—moved to Bishopville and lived nearby in an apartment, and then in a nursing home two blocks from Frances. As Marcia put it, "between her mother, mother-in-law, three daughters, husband, two dogs, one cat and the store, Frances kept busy." Frances was also active in Bishopville town life, becoming a member of the Kiwanis Club, Chamber of Commerce, Bridge Club, Shanghai Club, and American Legion.

Offspring of Frances and Arthur Ginsberg (2007). Sitting: John Lande, Beverly Ginsberg Lande, Nancy Ginsberg Thornton, Eamon Thornton and Sally Ginsberg Waters (inset). Standing: Sid Lande, Frances, Ken Lande.

In 1988, Frances's husband, Arthur, passed away suddenly. "He had walked around the block, and fell, and that was it," said Frances as she recalled the shocking death two decades later.[179] After Arthur's death, Frances, with help later from her oldest daughter, Nancy, kept the store going. By 2008, however, it was impossible to keep going—not because Frances lacked the energy, but because there just wasn't enough business. "[Bishopville] used to be a real bustling place," said Nancy, "Now it's just a lot of trucks coming through and nobody stops. You can't make a living.... Mom and Pop shops are a thing of the past right now and that's

---

179 "Closing of Bishopville Store Won't Slow Owner," WIS TV News, http://www.wistv. com/Global/story.asp?S=7840130 (accessed 11/11/2009).

sad."[180] And so, Frances reluctantly closed the store she had nurtured for many decades. Frances remains active, keeping in touch with her three daughters and traveling with them when she gets the opportunity.

Marcia remains in Cheltenham Township, outside Philadelphia. She was a stay-at-home mom until 1982, when she and Hy divorced after 28 years of marriage. After that, Marcia took a job as a legal secretary, from 1982-1995, before being forced to "retire" when her law firm downsized.

**Brody family (1976). Roslyn, Neal, Marcia
and Alan, with Hy behind them.**

Marcia has been involved in local politics, working as a Democratic Committee Person for ten years in Cheltenham, where she lives. A deputy constable at the polls on election days, she once ran, unsuccessfully, against an incumbent Commissioner who'd been in office for 30 years. Marcia, who is a life member of Hadassah, served as President for two years of the Hanna Senesch group of Hadassah.

---

180 *Id.*

Marcia is also the family historian, writing and distributing a family newsletter that goes to 58 families in 14 states, which keeps extended Bass family members up on the latest births, deaths, marriages, bar and bat mitzvahs, honors and awards among their number.[181]

One of Marcia's favorite hobbies is entering sweepstakes, from which she has won a number of prizes. The biggest was a sports package that included all expense paid trips to the Super Bowl, college basketball Final Four, and World Series.

Marcia also appeared on Bill Cosby's "You Bet Your Life" television show in 1993. According to Marcia, "[M]y son called and said they were going to audition people for the show. My Aunt Sadye, who is no longer living, told me, 'Always have one hand on your coat and one hand on the doorknob!' so when someone says, 'Do you want to go?', then I go! There was a whole room full of people at the audition. They asked people to speak on any subject for three minutes. I talked about myself. That's all I had to talk about."[182]

Selected for the show based on her audition, Marcia spent much of the segment telling Cosby about growing up in North, drawing many laughs. In May 2010 one of her nephews put the video clip on YouTube, where it became a sensation, receiving more than 5 million hits as it spread to other websites as well. Among the tens of thousands of viewer comments, one said, "Absolutely priceless. This woman is a jewel." Another wrote, "She is sweet and pleasant, knows how to hold her own. You just have to love her."[183]

Lucille still lives in Beaufort, a community fixture there, just like Frances in Bishopville. Her son Neil stayed in Beaufort and built his own shoe store across the street from the original Lipsitz Department Store. In 2002, the Lipsitz family hosted a lavish 100-year party and widely-reported commemoration of the department store. Two blocks of downtown's Bay Street were closed for the ceremony, attended by

---

181 As a child, Marcia was a pack rat, saving everything—autographed photos of movie stars she had written to, school papers, report cards, letters, written thoughts and goals—in a shoebox. Her mother threw it all away after becoming senile.

182 Sally McInerney, "Hearsay," *Anderson Independent Mail*, Jan. 17, 2011, available at http://www.independentmail.com/news/2011/jan/17/hearsay-ok-yall-lets-get-tuned---or-youre-doghouse/ (accessed Feb. 4, 2011).

183 See www.youtube.com/watch?v=nGRKTkS7pW8.

more than a thousand people, many from out of state. Lucille and Joe have hundreds of letters they've received over the years from friends and well-wishers around the world who've visited Beaufort at one time or another and stopped by their store.

Beaufort has also served as the backdrop for a number of feature films, including "The Big Chill," "Forrest Gump," and "Something To Talk About." The store can be seen in some of those movies, and many pieces of period clothing used in them—shoes, dresses, lingerie—originated in years-old stock stored in Lipsitz Department Store.

Just like Nathan Bass, the Lipsitz family has often taken in relatives and others passing through Beaufort. One year, Lucille's nephew Ken— her brother Jack's oldest son—spent the summer at the Lipsitz home while he and Lucille's son Barry, both in high school at the time, worked together in a nearby vegetable packing plant to earn money for a trip to Israel. The sea islands surrounding Beaufort are home to many truck farms growing cucumbers, tomatoes, green peppers and other vegetables that need to be packed and shipped during the summer, so Ken and Barry got a good lesson in manual labor. While with the Lipsitz's for the summer, Ken enjoyed the family pastimes, such as bingo and bowling, as well their large collection of exotic fish in the room in which he slept.

Lipsitz Family (1997). Sitting: Joe and Lucille. Standing: Sandra Lipsitz Mendel, Judy Lipsitz Thornberry, Neil and Barry.

Lucille enjoys baking and trying out new recipes (a trait, perhaps, from her namesake, Grandma Laske). Lucille, who saves everything, jokes that her children will remember her for at least 20 years after she passes on because it will take that long for them to sort through everything she has collected. Lucille was an extra in the movies "Forrest Gump" and "The Great Santini," and earned a mention in novelist Pat Conroy's book *Beach Music.* Lucille and Joe celebrated their 50th anniversary in January 2005.

In March, 2009, Lucille decided it was time to close Lipsitz Department Store and retire. Joe, was suffering from Alzheimer's and Lucille had been running the store on her own. "The store has been part of downtown Beaufort forever," said Lucille, "but it's just too much for me here by myself."[184] The store had been in the same location on Beaufort's Bay Street—its picturesque main street—for 107 years. The local newspaper described a stroll through the store as "like a trip through a time machine, taking a customer back to the days when mannequins modeled Buster Brown and Red Goose shoes and ladies bought boxed lingerie wrapped in tissue paper."[185] With the closing, another small-town Jewish store in the South had disappeared, but Lucille's son, Neil, for awhile continued the tradition with his shoe store across the street from where the Lipsitz Department Store stood for so many years.

The youngest of Nathan and Esther's children, Jack, went on to a distinguished career as a journalist and historian. After finishing his service in the Navy, Jack worked for a year on the copy desk of Charleston's daily newspaper. He edited reporters' stories, laid out page designs, wrote headlines, placed photographs and drafted cutlines (the press term for captions). The schedule was difficult, working Thursdays through Mondays until midnight or 2 a.m., often getting late breaking stories such as the birth of John F. Kennedy, Jr., in the next morning's paper.

After a year there, he and a close friend from college, Dew James, opened a weekly newspaper—the *West Ashley Journal*--in suburban Charleston. It was only at that point that he decided definitely against a career as sports writer. As Jack put it, he chose "to forego what a mature sports editor—whose column I read while stationed in San Diego—had referred to as the 'toy department' of the newspaper." After a few years, Jack sold the newspaper and moved to Columbia, where he worked as a journalist for the local newspapers, and later as the Columbia bureau chief for the *Charlotte Observer*. While working in Columbia, Jack was honored with a Nieman Fellowship—a prestigious program for journalists—for study at Harvard University in 1965-66.

In 1968, while working for the *Observer*, Jack covered a series of campus protests at all-black South Carolina State College in Orangeburg, 18 miles from North. The protests started when students challenged a

---

184 " Landmark Beaufort Store Says Farewell," *Island Packet*, http://www.island-packet.com/news/local/story/774704.html (accessed 11/11/2009)
185 *Id.*

local bowling alley owner's refusal to allow "colored" students to use its facilities. This was four years after passage of the Civil Rights Act had outlawed such discrimination in places of public accommodation. The protest quickly spread and became larger. The Governor called in the virtually all-white state highway patrol and National Guard troops. On the third night of protests, patrolmen, who had been issued deadly buckshot, opened fire, killing three students and wounding another 28. The shooting took place near the edge of the college campus.

The lethal shooting of students on a college campus shocked Jack, but the national media paid little attention—unlike the massive coverage generated two years later when four white students were shot and killed in daylight at Kent State University in Ohio. Local news reports were quite distorted, making it appear that the police had fired in self-defense against an angry mob, with the Associated Press inaccurately reporting "an exchange of gunfire." Jack reported the unfolding aftermath for months in the *Charlotte Observer* and decided the full story needed to be told. He took a leave of absence from his newspaper job and paired up with *Los Angeles Times* reporter Jack Nelson, who had also been writing in depth about the story, to write his first book, *The Orangeburg Massacre*, which has become accepted by historians as the definitive account of what happened.

Jack Bass the author.

Jack also earned the award for South Carolina "Newspaperman of the Year" in both 1968 and 1970, in part for his coverage of the Orangeburg story, but also for his unbiased coverage of other racially-charged events during that divisive period.

From there Jack went on to write a number of books, some co-authored, about southern political history and culture, including *Unlikely Heroes*, a chronicle of four federal appellate judges in the South who enforced the Supreme Court's decisions on race following Brown v. Board of Education; *The Transformation of Southern Politics*, an update of V.O. Key's classic analysis of the southern political scene in *Southern Politics in State and Nation*; *Taming The Storm*, a biography, edited by Jacqueline Onassis, of Federal Judge Frank Johnson in Alabama, who had courageously upheld the law against overwhelming white opposition; and a pair of biographies of legendary South Carolina governor and Senator Strom Thurmond—one before, and one after his death. The first served as Jack's Ph.D. dissertation in 1998 at Emory University. *Taming The Storm* won Jack the Robert F. Kennedy Book Award, including a reception at Ethel Kennedy's Virginia home that his four sisters all attended.

In 1978, Jack ran for Congress, and in the process managed to help his home town of North. During the campaign (he received 43 percent of the vote against incumbent Republican Floyd Spence), Jack learned from Mayor Mutt Livingston that North was seeking a $100,000 federal grant to fund a needed replacement for the town's water tower. From his political reporting, Jack knew key staff members for Senators Strom Thurmond and Fritz Hollings, called them about the situation, and sought their help—knowing that although the senators shared a mutual dislike for one another, their staffs worked together on matters affecting South Carolina. Jack learned from a Senate staffer that North's application for a grant, instead of being behind 40 others, had moved to the top. When North subsequently got the grant, Jack was quietly pleased that his campaign had made a difference for his home town. In those days, such grants weren't known as "earmarks."

In 1984, Jack and Carolyn were divorced. Jack remarried twice, first to poet Alice Cabaniss, and then in 1994 to Nathalie Dupree. Nathalie, a graduate of London's Cordon Bleu cooking school, is the author of ten cookbooks, two of them winners of prestigious James Beard awards, and has hosted more than 300 television cooking programs.

Jack Bass offspring (2004). Front row: Rachel Bass, David's wife Bonnie, and Liz's husband Joel Broadway holding daughter Ginny. Middle row: Jack, his wife Nathalie Dupree, and Jack's children David, Liz Bass Broadway, and Ken. Back row: Ken's son Danny, David's son Jacob, Ken's wife Catherine Wang, Ken's son Aidan, David's daughter Sarah and Liz's daughter Anna.

Jack continues to write and do commentary on politics. He has taught at South Carolina State College, the University of South Carolina, the University of Mississippi, the College of Charleston, and most recently at his deceased brother Herbert's alma mater, The Citadel, where he directed an oral history project to preserve the memories of that college's surviving WWII veterans. Jack is also the co-author of *The Palmetto State: The Making of Modern South Carolina*, the featured book in the USC Press 2009 Spring catalogue.

XXVIII. The New North

On July 1, 1992, Marcia, Ruth and Frances returned to North for a visit. "I felt like Rip Van Winkle, waking up after more than 30 years," said Marcia, who had been the furthest away for all those years. It was nearly 62 years to the day from the Fourth of July in 1930 on which Nathan Bass had returned to town with his oldest children from Lowell, Massachusetts to resume his work as a small town merchant.

Even small towns change over time. North was far different than it had been in the girls' childhood. The cotton platform was gone; the train depot was gone; the North Hotel was gone. Gone too was the old family home, which had been destroyed in a fire, as well as the garage, the barn, the chicken coop, the pecan trees and the fig tree. Their school, now fully integrated, had been mostly rebuilt around the original auditorium. The exterior, interior, and layout of what had been the old Bass Mercantile Store were completely different.

North had moved forward with the times. It now had a Town Hall with flowers blossoming in front. The new, racially integrated school had a real gymnasium. The town had a restaurant and a branch of the Orangeburg County public library. Green grass was growing where the cotton platform had been. One reassuring piece of continuity, however, was the Nelson-Bass American Legion Post, named after the sisters' brother Herbie and the town's other WWII casualty, Manning Nelson, son of the town's doctor—both graduates of The Citadel.

Politics in North has changed, too. It's been several decades since the public schools were desegregated. African-Americans, who form a majority in surrounding Orangeburg County, vote in elections. They've literally changed the face of the County's political structure, which now included many blacks, including a majority on the Orangeburg County Council.

More recently, on October 4, 2009, Frances, Marcia, Lucille and Jack attended a reunion of all North High School classes between 1940-1952.

More than 100 members and spouses of those classes (which ranged in size from 9 to 27) showed up, some from as far away as California.

The organizers prepared a program for the event, which provides a sociological report of the World War II students of North High School. Of the 149 living graduates (94 were deceased) of these 11 classes, more than 80 percent remained in South Carolina. Of those living in the state, almost a fourth still had North addresses. Another third resided nearby in either Orangeburg or Lexington Counties, with 18 having Orange-burg addresses.

The son of one of the participants, who acted as the official photographer, was kind enough to follow the Bass siblings to the Nelson-Bass American Legion Post, where he snapped photos of them both inside at the photo of Herbie and outside by the Nelson-Bass Legion Post sign beneath a waving American flag.

Jack recorded the event for the Times and Democrat, whose publisher, Cathy Culler Hughes, was the great grand-daughter of the Culler family with whom Nathan boarded during his first years in North, and the daughter of Zack Culler, shown in the background of the photo with Nathan Bass and Clarence Culler displaying their tomatoes for sale and shipment. Jack wrote of the reunion that at the end of the day, "everyone left with good memories, counting their blessings, and looking at the future."[186]

There aren't any Jewish families in North today, which is too bad. How will North's children be exposed to funny tasting chopped liver and matzah, to strange sounding Yiddish and Brooklyn accents, to unusual visitors from afar? The Bass family is long gone, but life goes on, and Jack and Nathalie regularly stop there for gas on their shortcut route when driving from Charleston to Atlanta. The memories remain.

---

186 Jack Bass, "North classes from 1940 to 1952 make the most of a special day," Orangeburg Times & Democrat online (10/10/09) http://www.thetandd.com/news/article_59ed808a-cbd0-5535-9083-a6a6407d13d3.html. Reprinted in Appendix.

Jack, Frances, Marcia and Lucille, in North for a joint class high school reunion, outside the Nelson-Bass American Legion Post.

Appendix

North classes from 1940 to 1952 make the most of a special day

By Jack Bass. The Times and Democrat | Posted: Saturday, October 10, 2009 1:00 am

NORTH, S.C. — My sister Marcia, who lives in Philadelphia, once got on Bill Cosby's "You Bet Your Life" TV show by explaining that she was from North, South Carolina, and that "North is 90 miles southeast of Due West," which of course is nothing but geographic fact.

She called me a month or two ago in Charleston and my sisters Lucille in Beaufort and Frances in Bishopville and said we should all get together and go to a reunion the first Saturday in October of all North High School classes between 1940 and 1952. We readily agreed. The original classes had ranged in size from nine to 27, and more than 100 people showed up — including three graduates who came in from California. Lively conversation followed, and a few ancient grudges were resolved.

There was so much hugging and hand-shaking going on that you'd never know that swine flu was out there. John D. Flake — known to all as John D. — got knowing smiles when he said one widowed friend had told him that all the eligible men she'd met "were looking for nurses and purses — and she wasn't interested."

Two members of the class of 1950, Gloria Robinson of North and Idalyn McCormick Spradling of Orangeburg — together with John D. — had planned in detail a similar event four years ago in Orangeburg. Those who attended had a good time, but when it was over, Spradling recalled Saturday, "Gloria and I said we would never do it again."

But months later their classmate Herbert Lynch of Hesperia, Calif., whose father had died while school superintendent in North for several of those graduating classes, contacted them to say he had been unable to attend and wanted them to plan another one.

He persisted. "I missed the last time," he said Saturday. "I hadn't seen classmates in 59 years." Lynch retired after 30 years working for the Department of Defense Overseas School System for children of American servicemen stationed overseas, much of it as a school principal in Europe.

The two women again planned everything, assisted by John. D., and with help from his wife of more than 50 years, Shirley — my next-door neighbor growing up and now a renewed friendship that began when I was 4 and she was 3. They produced a 40-page printed program with names, addresses and phone numbers for each class. They also arranged catering for a mouth-watering meal that included three desserts.

Some fully sampled each one, including a chocolate treat that appeared incapable of being eaten with any leftovers on the paper plate. Members of each class sat together at individual tables swapping stories and exchanging remembrances.

The program provides a sociological report of the World War II students of North High School. Of the 149 living graduates (94 are deceased) of these 11 classes, more than 80 percent remain in South Carolina. Of those living in the state, almost a fourth still have North addresses. Another third reside nearby in either Orangeburg or Lexington counties, with 18 having Orangeburg addresses.

The entire group lined up outside the North Baptist Church activity center for a photograph, and separate photographs were taken of each year's class group.

By the time everyone departed at 3:30 on Saturday, Marcia was saying, "It brings back all the memories of North. It's seeing people that you haven't seen in 65 years." Her classmate Joe Leaphart, who now lives in Greenville and whom she had not seen since their graduation in 1944, told her he still remembered "how you used to write so small." Until then she later said, "I didn't even know I wrote small."

The largest of the 11 classes (there was no graduation class in 1948 because that was the year South Carolina public schools expanded from 11 to 12 grades) was 1950 with 27 graduates.

As everyone was finishing dessert, a question was asked whether there should be another reunion in a few years. The response was overwhelmingly in favor, with strong appreciation expressed for the work of Gloria and Idalyn —and John D. too.

With that focus on the future, the people attending all understood that life has an end. Gloria had informed them in brief opening comments that one member of the class of 1947 had called a week earlier to say how excited he was about coming to the reunion. He died a few days later. Another who planned to attend had a medical emergency that required surgery to implant a stent; his doctor advised him to stay home. The group listened in silent understanding when John D. soberly commented, "I know I'm not getting any younger."

But everyone left with good memories, counting their blessings, and looking at the future. They now await receipt in a few days of a DVD from which they can select prints from a large number of photographs taken by Gloria's son, Billy Robinson. He also was kind enough to follow me and my sisters to the Nelson-Bass American Legion Post — named for our brother Herbert and his friend Manning Nelson, two Citadel graduates killed in action during World War II — and taking photographs of the four of us beside the Legion Post sign outside and beneath the American flag waving above.

The final stanza of the North High School alma mater printed on the back cover of the program summed up the day:

May it ever be our watch word
Conquer and prevail,
Hail to thee our Alma Mater.
Dear ole North High hail.

North native Jack Bass is co-author of The Palmetto State, the featured book in the University of South Carolina Press 2009 summer catalog.
http://www.thetandd.com/news/article_59ed808a-cbd0-5535-9083-a6a6407d13d3.html

www.ingramcontent.com/pod-product-compliance
Lightning Source LLC
Chambersburg PA
CBHW062201280526
45788CB00001B/396